TRANSFORMING ANXIETY

FROM HOT MESS TO SUPERPOWER

Transforming Anxiety
From Hot Mess to Superpower

ISBN: 978-1-7782335-0-0

www.ToddKaufman.ca

A Canadian production

Dedicated to my many clients: Over the years, you have had the courage to keep showing up, determined to make your life better.

Being a part of your life change changed me. You helped me deepen my compassion, stretch my skills and keep learning how to be better as both a person and professional.

A special thank you to those of you who joined me early in this journey. You hung in there and we figured it out together. And because we did, thousands of lives have been changed!

Every smile, hug, letter and referral has meant so much to me. Life is a journey to be enjoyed, not stressed over. I feel both honoured and blessed to have shared this journey with you.

This book is not intended to replace your doctor or therapist. For some people, panic attacks and anxiety may be best treated by skilled medical practitioners. I encourage you to seek medical advice if you believe you need it, and invite you to use this book in conjunction with the advice from your medical practitioner or therapist, as they recommend. The Anxiety Release Protocol (ARP) is a carefully crafted, structured integration of various therapeutic modalities, and it is taught worldwide to practitioners wanting to specialize in anxiety and stress-related treatments. This book does not constitute a cure.

TRANSFORMING ANXIETY
From Hot Mess to Superpower

TRANSFORMING ANXIETY

FROM HOT MESS TO SUPERPOWER

Todd Kaufman, BA, BFA, MDiv
Psychotherapist, Anxiety Specialist,
and Former Anxiety Sufferer

You are about to meet a number of my clients and friends who have transformed their anxiety from a hot mess into their superpower!

I have carefully selected a few key stories to share with you from the hundreds of people that the Anxiety Release Protocol has helped.

In order to protect their privacy, names and details have been changed, but the truth of their stories remains.

Introduction

There are few things more unsettling than being the focus of over 500 wedding guests, all of whom have the same question you do: "What happened to the bride?"

On a lovely spring day, I was wrapping up a fun and incredibly engaging day of teaching fellow therapists and doctors the Anxiety Release Protocol (ARP), a program I had developed to help people end panic attacks and manage anxiety. The classroom was lined with handwritten flip-chart sheets, each filled with notes reviewing the day's work. Everyone in the workshop had bonded, and as they were saying their final goodbyes I began to collect the large sheets peppered with key thoughts and strategies.

"Excuse me, Todd?" A twenty-something social worker named Sarah was approaching me. She had arrived that morning expecting only to sit quietly in a back-row seat and watch. But as the day unfolded, she had become engaged and quite animated. By the end of the day, Sarah had moved herself front and centre. She was a petite woman, perhaps five-foot-four, with a warm, open face and big, saucer-like eyes. A broad smile had replaced the morning's shyness, and when she directed that smile your way, it simply made you feel loved. “Thank you, I learned so much today. I really think it’s going to help my clients. A lot of them have panic attacks and, well, as you know, so do I. But the best part is the fact that I had so much fun. I don’t usually expect that when I come to a workshop!”

I smiled and thanked Sarah for her words. Feedback like that always feels like a gift.

Sarah continued, “I’m wondering if I could ask a rather personal favour?”

I nodded, presuming that what might come next was a request to work together in some capacity.

“Will you marry me?”

As my face registered surprise and confusion, Sarah exclaimed, “No, no—wait! What I mean is, will you officiate my wedding?”

We both began to laugh. I remembered that I had in fact mentioned at some point during the day that I was licensed to officiate weddings in Canada. “Of course!” I said. “I’d love to.”

Eight months later, there I was, standing in front of 500 of Sarah’s family and friends in an impressive banquet hall, groomsmen to my left, and Dan, a very nervous groom, at my side. Dan was breaking a sweat and rather desperately looking about the room for his (hopefully!) soon-to-be wife. We had been waiting there far too long for anyone to be comfortable.

I reached out, touched Dan’s shoulder and smiled in an attempt to reassure him. Then, facing the guests, I said, “Ladies and gentlemen, we apparently have a small technical problem. Please give me a moment, and we will begin the wedding shortly.” For the sake of all present, and particularly my now terrified groom, I hoped the words I had spoken to the room were true.

As I proceeded down the aisle, I could hear my shoes clicking on the marble floors and echoing in the massive expanse of the wedding hall above the shuffling and the murmurs. I had not checked in on the bride prior to the wedding. At Dan’s and Sarah's request, they wanted to uphold the tradition of her not being seen by a man on their wedding day until she walked down the aisle to take his hand in marriage.

I exited the wedding hall and rushed across the massive reception area to a small room I understood to be the bridal suite. I could hear some commotion on the other side of the door and knocked gently.

There was no answer.

I knocked again, placed my hand on the door handle and gently opened the door.

There, on the floor, in a pile of lace, crinoline and tears, was Sarah. The bride was surrounded by her bridesmaids, her mom and a whole group of female relatives desperately trying to help her.

Sarah was in the middle of massively freaking out, and the women around her were telling her to calm down. No one in the history of freaking out has ever calmed down by being told to calm down.

Sarah was gasping for breath and through her sobs was asking for an ambulance. She'd had these attacks before, but never like this. Sarah was quite convinced that this time she was indeed having a heart attack.

My entrance was met with hope but also concern that a man had just breached the sanctity of the girls-only event. As a therapist and coach specializing in anxiety, I had no doubt what was going on. Sarah was in a flat out, 10-out-of-10 panic attack.

"Could everyone please leave the room and give me just a few minutes with Sarah?" I knew how to solve this, and I needed 10 minutes alone with the bride to do it. But I might as well have been asking a mother bear to step away from her cubs. "OK, I really do know how to fix this. I'm a therapist. I understand what's going on here, and I really want to give Sarah a chance to get married today. I can do this. But I really need to talk to Sarah alone."

Slowly, the women began to rise, and as they headed for the exit, many of them placed their hand on my arm offering their words of wisdom, or veiled threats that I had better not mess with their little girl!

As the door clicked shut with the exit of the final bridesmaid, I got down on my knees in front of Sarah. My arrival hadn't exactly calmed her down, but I was just getting started. I locked eyes with her. "Sarah, I know what this is. This is what I do. You are having a panic attack. Panic attacks are incredibly uncomfortable, but they are not dangerous."

She looked at me, those big eyes filled with tears. Between sobs, Sarah uttered a broken, "Are you sure? I think I need an ambulance."

"No, Sarah. You're going to be fine. Panic attacks are extremely uncomfortable but they're not dangerous. You've had this before and have you ever died from it?" I took her hands. "Sarah, do you want to get married today?" Before I did anything, I wanted to make sure that Sarah was truly prepared to commit herself to a life with Dan.

Through all the tears and panic, Sarah nodded and said, "Yes."

"OK—then Sarah, I want you to pay really close attention to me. I want you to repeat everything I say and everything I do. Can you do that?"

Again, Sarah nodded.

I come from a family of girls, the exceptions being me, of course, as well as my awesome dad and a wonderful black Lab named Monty who was the constant companion of my youth. All four of us kids were born about five years apart, and I was the third child. As is seemingly incumbent upon all big brothers, I often showed my kid sister, Leasa, how much I loved her by tormenting her. One very effective strategy I used—one that all big brothers know—was to follow her around the house and repeat everything she said and did. As effective a strategy as it was, it would consistently meet its demise when she, usually in tears, would run to our mother complaining, "Mom! Todd is saying everything I say!" It was a complaint that I would immediately parrot, only to suffer the inevitable consequences from an irritated parent.

It was a rather primal game but also one that I was now asking Sarah to play. If she had a big brother, she may well have refused to participate. But she agreed, so I got to work.

Ten minutes later, Sarah stood up, patted the tears from her face and took my hand while I escorted her back to the wedding hall. At the entrance we stopped. I gave her a gentle hug, turned, and with all eyes on me, my footsteps again echoed with a loud click...click...click as I walked down the aisle to the nervously waiting wedding party.

I smiled warmly at a visibly relieved groom and turned to face Dan and Sarah's family and friends. Stretching my arms wide in invitation, I asked, "Ladies and gentlemen, please stand for the entrance of the bride!" The music shifted, the guests stood in unison, and a beautiful, smiling Sarah glided down the aisle, past 500 guests, and took her groom's hand.

Sarah and Dan turned to face me, and only minutes after she had been certain her life was in jeopardy Sarah married the man of her dreams.

It All Starts Here

So let us begin. This book is the answer to ending panic attacks and managing anxiety. It contains the strategy I used with Sarah in that bridal suite and much more. I did not tell you her story to impress you, I told it to impress *upon* you that what you are about to read and learn *works*.

This book will teach you the *Anxiety Release Protocol.* I developed the ARP over many years through working with hundreds of clients. This protocol is an amalgamation of many techniques presented in a very specific structure to give you the necessary foundation for ending panic attacks and managing your anxiety. You might have heard of some of the ideas and techniques in this book, such as mindful meditation and breathing exercises. You might have even tried them with some degree of success. ARP takes the best and most effective elements of each of the exercises and integrates them into a unique approach that simply *works*.

A few quick notes before we begin. Regardless of your previous experience with any strategies you encounter in this book, your success with the ARP depends on you reading even these sections with an open mind. You might discover a new way of looking at something you've tried before, or a different and more powerful way of doing it. If you have experience in any one technique and it works for you, keep it up, but please do not skip the section in this book that addresses the technique. You will find it presented and practiced in a unique way that, as a part of this program, will help you achieve a life free of panic attacks and out-of-control anxiety.

Second, this book is carefully structured to walk you through the ARP lessons and insights step-by-step. ARP's approach is unique. Your success will depend on walking through the program in the manner it is presented. If you miss how all these bits and pieces are presented, you might not get the same results so many others have.

On this journey of discovery, you're likely to encounter exercises and concepts that might seem a little esoteric (or "woo-woo," if I may borrow a term popular with skeptics). If you, like me, have a traditional Western education or even clinical training in your background, your worldview might lead you to think less of these solutions.

In fact, my experience has taught me that the more invested a person is in clinging to their worldview as *the* right and valid way to access and process the world, the more likely they are to experience panic attacks and anxiety. The universe has a way of poking through our "being right," and when it does we can become shaken and can experience extreme anxiety and panic. (Oddly, that can even mean that the smarter we are, the more difficult it can be for us to learn new things.)

As you read through the protocol, if you encounter ideas that don't make sense to the way you see the world, that confuse you or even trigger an angry response, keep in mind that these are all the cues that you need consider suspending your worldview for a few moments while you engage a new idea. It might be only that the language used for something familiar is different from what you're used to reading. For example, what one person calls "the power of meditation," another might call "the power of prayer." Perhaps, in essence, they are talking about the same concept. Or you might really dislike religion or "spiritual" stuff, and your mind throws up a big wall whenever either of those words come up, preventing you from learning something new and powerful.

When you can suspend your worldview long enough to be curious, you can learn great things. And remember: To *suspend* your worldview does not mean to *give up* your worldview; it just means that when you notice the dissonance you can be smart enough and curious enough to keep digging and look for the lesson.

Some years ago, I interviewed a well-known quantum physics researcher at a major American university. He told me that the most difficult thing he had learned in his decades of research was that the ideas at the very core of how he had learned to conduct scientific research no longer held up in the field of quantum physics. For decades, the formula for research had been to propose a hypothesis and then set out to carefully prove or disprove it. The researcher came to learn that this method did not always work; his recent discoveries were so shocking that his hypotheses didn't even make sense to the classically trained mind. He described his most recent hypothesis as akin to asking, "Is this chair married?" The newest discoveries in his field had forced him to rethink how he approached science, and only because of his stature and previous accomplishments did his contemporaries not consider him crazy. You might find at moments while learning the ARP that you feel a little like this professor once did, trying to force his groundbreaking discoveries in quantum physics into a scientific method that was no longer up to the job.

Because I believe you are reading this book because you really *do* want answers, either to help yourself or to help others, I need something very important from you in order to make this work. I need to ask you to consider an absolutely critical concept:

Exchange being right for being curious.

Embracing curiosity is how you begin to *learn*. And let's be honest here: If what you already know about ending panic attacks and managing anxiety worked, you probably wouldn't be reading this book!

This critical request is maybe the hardest thing I am going to ask you to do. Think about it; talk to your friends about it; stretch your comfort zone in the safety of a conversation with a wise therapist: Do what it takes to replace being *right* with being *curious*. I've helped people through ARP many, many times, and I know with great certainty that your journey to a panic-free life with anxiety management must begin here. After all, what you are about to read isn't just theory; it is a set of real-life, tried and true techniques. (One of my favourite T-shirts reads, "Well that is all well and good in practice, but how does it hold up in theory!")

The ARP and its embedded techniques *work*. I have personally counselled hundreds of people using the ARP in the very same manner you are about to experience. The only difference is that I am not sitting next to you in person. I wrote this book for you in a manner that I believe will compensate for the fact that you and I aren't doing this together in real time.

That might leave you with an important question, one I should answer before asking you to take this journey with me.

Who am I?

It's Time We Met

Have you ever noticed how many people, when asked who they are, answer with their name and profession? Or if not their profession, something else top of mind and important to them. I've been known to respond, "Hi, I'm Todd, Gracey's dad!" (Gracey is my wonderful mixed-breed dog, who is trained to work in my clinic as a therapy aide.) Or I could say, "Hi, I'm Todd, a psychotherapist, coach and author." Or, in days long gone by I could have said, "Hi, I'm Todd, a yacht captain, a pastor, a banker, a real estate agent, or one of many other things. You see, I've gotten around a bit. My dad taught me to find what makes you happy, then find someone to pay you for it. (Dad likely should have included, "and keep it vertical and legal!" Which I must add, I have.) My career path has been driven by my passions. Ultimately, I realized that behind all of what I had done was a calling to care for people and make the world a bit better place.

Back in the early 1980's I lived in Toronto, Canada. My best friend, David, had received a diagnosis that had left him with a very short time to live. We gathered up all my airline points and took off for one last trip together. We headed to Australia via Hawaii and Fiji. David only made it to Fiji before he became too sick to continue. At his request, I took the rest of our combined funds, packed him on a flight home and continued our adventure—alone. His parting gift: "Don't try to call me before you get home." This took place long before social media existed, so there would be no news as to his wellness.

When I came home many weeks later, it took me a ton of

courage to finally pick up the phone and call David. A mutual friend answered his phone. David was still alive—but barely. A care team was in place and I instantly dove in to help. Control freak that I was, I stepped up to organize others, find food services, search out free medication, voluntary nurses and more. It was a full-on battle and I was going to lead the charge. Some part of me believed the more I kept busy, the longer David would live.

Within a month of my return, David's beleaguered body could fight no more. It was a quiet, snowy afternoon and I had fallen asleep in a chair next to his bed. I had slumped over and my head was resting next to David's chest. A light tap on my should woke me. "Todd, David is dead." It was the day nurse.

My flurry of activity continued: wake, funeral, thank you cards and more. And then it stopped. And then I crumbled. I had been in such high gear for so long, and now I felt so alone. Moments of panic would grip me as I went about mundane tasks. At 2:04 am every night, I would wake with a start.

It took me a while to understand I was suffering from anxiety and panic attacks. I sought help from doctors, therapists, psychiatrists and others. Slowly I figured out what my body was trying to tell me every time my anxiety went into overdrive, allowing me to stop focusing on what was happening to me and start to focus on becoming the man I chose to be. And I chose to be someone who cared for others.

I dove into research and study, and I carried all I learned with me through my life of many careers. Ultimately, I decided to dedicate my life to teaching others how to do the very thing that allowed me to be the person I chose: manage their anxiety and end panic attacks. I studied to be a counsellor, then psychotherapist and coach. I worked with hundreds of people who struggled with anxiety and panic, and from this experience I developed the Anxiety Release Protocol. This book is just one way I hope to help you, and in turn I trust you will pass on these skills to others.

If, after reading this book and implementing the ARP, you want more support, reach out to me or a trained ARP therapist, and let's get you into some sort of one-on-one set-up.

But first, let's journey through the protocol together. If you really want to get it, I really want to share it with you. So read carefully and pretend I am right there with you!

Let's begin. And let's begin by being *curious*—about science, in our first chapter.

Just because you have a

THOUGHT

does not mean you
have to keep it.

Chapter One

YOU ARE NOT BROKEN – **MOTHER NATURE** SET YOU UP!

The Negative Evolutionary Bias

Charles Darwin, upon returning from his travels aboard the *Beagle,* was housebound for years with a gripping case of agoraphobia that left him terrified to go outside. Even one of the world's greatest scientific explorers was not exempt from anxiety. His insights from his voyage started a scientific revolution called *evolution*—and it is here that we should begin to understand how to stop our panic attacks and manage our anxiety.

Let me introduce to you to two cavemen, Brad and Larry. Brad was not the brightest caveman on the block. Larry, however, was a bit of a wily brute. They were neighbours.

Early one morning, Brad and Larry emerged from their caves to gather breakfast from the forest. Both noticed a rustle in the bushes. Larry, the ever-cautious caveman, always on the alert for danger, had brought his club with him that morning. Brad, never one to think ahead, was unarmed and moseyed on to pick a few berries.

The rustle in the bush was a tiger. Breakfast plans shifted! Empty-handed Brad became the tiger's breakfast, but well-armed Larry was able to defend himself and get away.

Fast forward a few millennia and humans have become the Earth's apex species. An apex species is simply the animal at the top of the food chain—master of the domain, so to speak. Just as the great white shark rules the ocean, we humans rule the planet. We've never run very fast, had huge fangs, a coat of armor or—my favourite form of self-defense—stunk like a skunk. Yet, here we are at the top. We managed this on account of Larry, not Brad. Brad was prehistoric cat food—and as a result we have zero DNA from our sweet-but-not-too-bright caveman. Larry, however, returned safely to his dwelling and, as a result, was able to have a great big family and pass on his DNA.

Humans evolved a keen ability to scan for and sense danger, and we use our well-developed cognitive skills to run those dangerous future scenarios through our heads to prepare for the safest possible outcome. Larry, who thought ahead and saw the possibility of tigers, was all over that, therefore so are we!

The region of our brain that is highly tuned to scan for and sense danger is a small almond-shaped segment called the *amygdala*. This small-but-powerful region has developed since the days of Larry so effectively that, combined with our ability to reason or think (done mostly in the front part of our brain called the pre-frontal cortex), it has kept enough of us safe for humans to become the planet's dominant species.

The amygdala is one of the few regions of your brain that is pretty much fully baked and ready to go at birth. Even a newborn child knows fear. Clap your hands or otherwise startle an infant and she will cry. Unfortunately, she does not have the neuronal or physical development to run or fight, but the urge is there and strong.

The amygdala, which does our emotional processing, works as a team with a part of our brain called the *hypothalamus*. The hypothalamus is a control centre that manages a whole pile of involuntary systems in our body like breathing and our heart rate. It is technically the hypothalamus that orders the release of our "fight or flight" hormones, adrenaline and cortisol, and it does so as a direct response to an alert from our amygdala. So as your brain continued to form after birth, there was this little amygdala, online and working furiously. And as you began to learn about your world and structure thoughts, this well-practiced part of your brain had a lot to say about how you think.

Fast forward to now and *presto*: You have inadvertently programmed yourself to create most of your thoughts from the part of your brain that is constantly scanning for danger. It reports to your pre-frontal cortex, which then starts formulating defense or avoidance strategies to keep you safe. It's important to note that, since all of the events your amygdala is constantly scanning for are in the future and have not actually happened, they are *fictional*. Once they are given to the thinking part of your brain to handle—the pre-frontal cortex—it works hard to run case scenarios as if they are real in order to protect you. How much time have you invested in running through case scenarios about how to have that talk with your partner, or how to avoid an uncomfortable or dangerous event? How many times have you said to yourself, *What if?*

As a result of this process, most of us take these ***F****ictional* ***E****vents* ***A****ppearing* ***R****eal* and ruminate on them, getting stuck in "thought loops" that are anxiety-provoking and may trigger a panic attack.

FEAR: Fictional Events Appearing Real

Understandably, if you are stuck with FEAR-based thinking, you are going to feel a great deal of anxiety!

Now all of this FEAR-based thinking sounds pretty unfortunate, if we skim past the fact that this way of thinking allowed us to evolve and stop being other species' breakfast. On many occasions this is *the very* thought process that has kept you alive. It is your good old amygdala that flushed you full of adrenaline and cortisol in under 1/12th of a second that got you to turn your head in the direction of that car horn, empowering you to sprint out of the way. (Please don't text and walk!) But, as useful as a rush of adrenaline can be when we're in danger, not every bush has a tiger in it. There's a big difference between being prepared for trouble, like caveman Larry, and living every moment as if that tiger is ready to strike.

Yup – It's All in Your Head!

Many of us are raised and educated in cultures that teach us to think a great deal about many things, but they often fail to teach us *how* to *think*. For many adults, the idea that they can create their own thoughts, change or discard unwanted thoughts, or do anything but endure whatever thoughts happen to fill their minds has never occurred to them. And if it has occurred to them, it did so as little more than a passing desire: "I wish this was not on my mind," "I can't stop thinking about this!" or "I've worried about this for so long I'm just sick about it!"

So how about this thought:

> "Just because you have a thought
> that does not mean you have to keep it."

You don't have to keep your thoughts! *How* you let go of, change, reframe or otherwise manage a thought is a learned skill—just like handwriting or learning to play baseball. (But fear not: No athletic inclination is required here!)

Thank science for discovering what those of us who have ended our panic attacks and unmanageable anxiety already know: Our brain has a "plastic" nature, which means we can change and train how it works. Science calls this *neuroplasticity*. We will be talking a fair bit about neuroplasticity in this book, as it is one of the essential keys to solving the problem of anxiety.

In the famous psychoanalyst Sigmund Freud's *Introductory Lectures on Psychoanalysis*, he foresaw just how important dealing with anxiety could prove to the study of how our minds work: "The problem of anxiety is a nodal point at which the most various important questions converge, a riddle that is bound to throw a flood of light on our whole mental existence." (This comment marks an evolution of his earlier suspicion that anxiety arose out of the surplus energy of an unfilled libido.) Indeed, the concept that we have the capacity to manage and choose our thoughts, long understood in many Eastern cultures, and the recent understanding of the plastic nature of our brain (neuroplasticity), really do shake up the way we view our mental existence, as Freud predicted.

So what this all means for you (perhaps right up to the very moment you are reading this chapter) is that most or even all of your thoughts are precipitated by—or at least heavily influenced by—your amygdala. And not unlike an over-protective helicopter parent, your amygdala is on high alert for any possible danger, real or imagined, and overly eager to kick into action.

What is so very exciting about all of this is that Freud was right: By learning to manage your anxiety, you are about to illuminate the mysterious workings of your own mind, showing you how to solve the riddle of anxiety and live a panic attack free life with a level of anxiety that is not a problem, but is actually helpful.

In fact, just by reading what you have, you have already begun this journey.

From Hot Mess to Superpower

There is an ancient legend that says the day may come when mother nature blinks, and it will all be over for us humans. Considering how we have treated her precious earth; one might say it was quite understandable! The power of nature is unfathomable, yet throughout our history man has tried to use science tame and conquer her—with limited results.

In the early 1900s the science of nuclear radiation and nuclear fission began to develop. Most of the research was focussed on building an atomic bomb. It was not until half a century later we began to harness this energy for the good of humanity to create power. If we find a way to harness any energy, nuclear or otherwise, the decision of how we use it, be it for good or evil, is up to us.

For those of you who have experienced an all-out ten out of ten panic attack, you know how much energy is involved. There is a reason some of us call it a 'meltdown!' That much energy let loose without an intentional focus can literally feel like we are melting down. Even lesser moments of anxiety hold an incredible amount of energy and can feel very overwhelming.

Imagine if you would, all that energy being focussed for good? Imagine that energy serving you as your superpower? Well, my friend, it has, and this book will show you how to make it happen again.

Remember those moments when you had that sneaky suspicion, that intuition, that heads-up, something was just not safe? Perhaps you were traveling and decided to not walk down a small lane, or quickly bailed on a first date, knowing this person was bad news? Or as a parent, your 'Spidey sense' may have tingled when your kids were in danger? There are stories of moms who lift a car to save their trapped child, and stories of others who showed super-human strength to save their own life.

It is the VERY SAME POWER, that can save a life, as can give you a panic attack! In fact, it is the same hormones that give a mom the power to lift a car, that gives you that feeling of a meltdown. All this energy has worked for good before in your life, and it can again. The difference between you now, and after you have mastered the Anxiety Release Protocol, is your ability to use this force for good in your life. You can learn to allow it to show up in ways it can be helpful and not harmful!

In many superhero stories, we meet the young superhero frightened and wary of their powers that have been wreaking havoc. Yet a mentor shows up at just the right time to teach them how to use those powers for good.

"For my ally is the Force, and a powerful ally it is!" —Yoda

The Anxiety Release Protocol will teach you how to use the force for good! So, let's continue as your turn has come!

No one in the history of

CALMING DOWN

ever calmed down by being told to calm down.

CALMING DOWN IS AN ART

not a yelling match.

Chapter Two

THE ANATOMY OF A **PANIC ATTACK**

You may never have suffered a panic attack—that all-out meltdown that can feel like you are dying (that is a very real feeling and you are about to learn why)—yet you may still experience high levels of anxiety. When that anxiety becomes such a problem that it interferes with your life, it is time to learn how to work with your brain's first responders to get better results.

Anxiety can impact you on a continuum: Sometimes anxiety can come as a slight passing feeling or, at its worst, you can find yourself in an emergency room convinced you are having a heart attack. As we learn how to end these panic attacks and manage anxiety I will often just refer to "anxiety attacks" or "panic attacks," different terms meaning the same terrifying spike in cortisol. Even these most alarming episodes fall on an anxiety continuum, so please understand when I refer to "anxiety" I am referring to any level of anxiety you personally consider uncomfortable, from those severe attacks to the less noticeable state of constantly raised cortisol.

In this chapter I want to share with you a few key understandings that will make a dramatic impact in the length and severity of any panic attack. I will begin with a story.

Many years ago, I trained in an inner-city hospital in a major city in the USA. The weekend shift in the emergency room was right out of a TV drama. And, despite what some may tell you, a Saturday night with a full moon was a guarantee for more drama than even a TV show could provide. Patients arrived not just in screaming ambulances; people wandered in looking for help, or were dragged in by friends and loved ones, whether they wanted to be there or not. The ER waiting room was always filled beyond capacity with people from all walks of life in need of urgent care. City police paced carefully through the crowds, as the metal detectors didn't always catch a gang member, there for help or for revenge, who slipped in with a gun or knife hidden in his belt or boot.

One particularly busy night, people were crying, yelling and demanding attention. Triage nurses behind bulletproof glass were doing their best to help the neediest first, carefully escorting them from the waiting room and through the two large glass-and-metal security doors, always minded by two armed cops.

Anyone would find this environment stressful, and Becky definitely did. She arrived with a suspected heart attack or at least cardiac distress, and so had been bumped to the top of the care list. She was quickly moved inside where a team of nurses, technicians and doctors descended upon her to make a fast call as to the likelihood of a life-threatening cardiac event.

Becky lay on a stretcher, surrounded tightly by this large group of medical professionals moving in a flurry while peppering her with questions about any family history of heart attacks. A doctor ripped her shirt open and attached a heart monitor. A nurse stuck an IV needle in her arm for the potential rapid delivery of meds and drew blood from her other arm for emergency screening. The whirlwind of activity was expertly orchestrated, but to Becky it was a terrifying cacophony of abrupt sounds, chemical smells, needle pokes and manhandling. Being inside the ER amongst the doctors and nurses was just as frightening to her as the waiting room, maybe even more so.

When doctors had all the data they needed and regular blood tests returned with no markers indicating heart distress, a kind but overworked nurse escorted Becky out of the much-needed triage room, down the hall and into my office: "Todd, this one is yours."

Badly shaken, Becky stepped hesitantly inside. I showed her to a seat. She was still struggling to breathe, and she was clutching her chest believing full well the doctors were wrong and this was the big one. She knew. She just knew in her gut she was dying.

With all the clinical evidence to the contrary, I knew what was really happening to Becky. Something had triggered her amygdala into a complete "red alert," as some of my clients like to call it. Becky's fight or flight system was in overdrive. She was having a panic attack.

Here's what was going on in Becky's body: In preparation to keep her safe, her amygdala had triggered her hypothalamus and it was flushing high levels of adrenaline, followed by cortisol, through her body. The first flush took less than 1/12th of a second. The hormones were causing her heart to beat faster to speed up the flow of blood to the major muscle groups in her legs and arms in order to prepare her to run for safety or do battle. Her muscles needed oxygenated blood, so the hormones gave her that feeling of not being able to breathe to encourage just the opposite: hyperventilation. All that oxygen-rich blood moved to her extremities, making her hands, feet and head feel warm and tingly.

The longer the process continued, the more dangerous it seemed to Becky and her amygdala. Becky was prepared to do anything to fight off the attack, and all her amygdala noticed was her intent to fight. So, in keeping with its duty to prep the body to run or fight, it released even more cortisol and the cycle continued to escalate. Since Becky and her amygdala were certain she was in imminent danger from which she needed to escape, her body was diverting resources away from such internal processes as filtering urine or digesting food.

Becky's internal organs were beginning to notice that oxygen-rich blood was being diverted to the extremities and that they were being critically short-changed. (Under different circumstances this shortage really could harm organs, but you'd need to be suffering from more medical complications than a panic attack for that to happen. The body has a very effective way of kicking in an emergency balancing system before damage occurs.) Our bodies are complex organisms that communicate well. Urgent signals were sent by Becky's blood-deficient organs to her brain screaming, "Hey, we are dying down here!" And there sat Becky, feeling as if she really were facing her impending death.

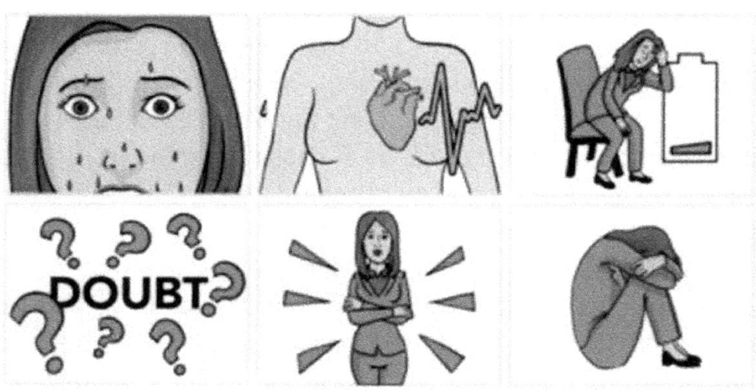

What you need to notice here...

is that the symptoms you may experience as an anxiety attack are more accurately described as the dependable outcome of having elevated cortisol levels in your body. It is the cortisol that causes all these symptoms. A simple cause and effect. Pump cortisol into your system, either by amygdala release or a syringe, and presto, you get an elevated heart rate, a sense of choking, tingly extremities, flushing and even a sense of impending death.

I moved close to Becky and took her hands. I made eye contact with her, squeezed her hands and told her with as much authority as I could muster (which is pretty substantial in these situations!) the first key to stepping out of the panic attack: "Becky, you are having a panic attack. Panic attacks are incredibly uncomfortable. Panic attacks are *not* dangerous."

I continued to hold her hands, which were gripping my own firmly now, and looked into her eyes. I repeated again, confidently: "Becky, you are having a panic attack. Panic attacks are incredibly uncomfortable. Panic attacks are *not* dangerous."

I could tell Becky's brain was beginning to process what I was saying. She was making brief eye contact and acknowledging that she was hearing me.

"Have you had these before?" I said.

She nodded. She was not yet able to catch her breath. "And they *always* end, don't they?"

Becky again nodded and she relaxed her grip.

"Have you ever woken up dead from one of these panic attacks?"

She tilted her head as part of her brain continued to panic while another part tried to devote resources to a question that seemed pretty ridiculous. She smiled a bit.

"Well, Becky," I continued, "You just managed to nail the motherlode of all panic attacks tonight. That must have felt a bit like a nuclear meltdown!" I laughed gently and Becky chuckled. (Laughter is clinically proven to lower cortisol levels.) "Good thing we are on the tail end of this one," I said, confirming for her vigilant brain that the danger, even if it was only perceived danger, was almost past.

I had just shared with Becky a second key to ending panic attacks: Panic attacks always come to an end.

Panic attacks always come to an end.

Becky became more grounded and present, behaving more like she was in a hospital with a therapist trying to help her instead of looking as if she were ready to bolt from some imagined threat. She began to settle. I encouraged her to smile and even laugh. Her amygdala finally decided the world was a safe place again and stopped ordering cortisol into her exhausted body. We spent a few minutes together learning one of the key techniques of the ARP that I'll explain in later chapters, and which would allow Becky to lower her cortisol at will. It was the same technique that saved the day for Sarah, our bride.

These are the first key things to really know, understand and internalize about anxiety attacks:

Panic attacks are incredibly uncomfortable; panic attacks are *not* dangerous. They don't last forever and always come to an end.

Becky went home not long after, escorted by her husband and daughter, with a referral in her hand to the best anxiety therapist I knew in the city.

Do you understand what I meant when I said, "know, understand and internalize?" You just read that "Panic attacks are incredibly uncomfortable; panic attacks are not dangerous." This is the third time I have shared this critical gem of information with you, and I have done so for a reason. It is one thing to *know* a fact, and it is another to *internalize* the knowing so deeply that it becomes your truth. When something is a *truth to you*, it becomes the first thought your mind creates whenever you think of an anxiety attack.

How we change a fact in our minds from being just information to being a deep form of knowing is exactly the same way we learn a new sport or master a musical instrument: We *intentionally rewire our brain*. The skill of changing our brain is called *neuroplastic change*. With every new thing we want to perfect or deeply know, there are three components to the neuroplastic change process. We are going to investigate making neuroplastic change in the next chapter.

It likely comes as no surprise to you that Becky had a history of anxiety and panic attacks. Until our meeting that day, when Becky and I were able to end her panic attack and I was able to provide her with helpful directions to prevent them from happening again, Becky had developed a firm conviction that all of her symptoms—elevated heart rate, the feeling that she couldn't breathe, tingling hands and feet, and even the feeling of impending death—were the symptoms of something more dangerous than a panic attack. This seems like a perfectly logical assumption, and most of us hold this assumption until we come to understand what we're going to discuss next.

The Culprits: Adrenaline and Cortisol

Bear with me here because we need to talk some endocrinology—the study of the endocrine system, which consists of all the glands that secrete hormones directly into your lymph system or bloodstream. You have been reading quite a bit already about two of these hormones. Anxiety attacks mainly involve *adrenaline* and *cortisol*.

Adrenaline is the hormone I've been talking about that rushes through our body in less than 1/12th of a second and gets us ready to respond to an impending dangerous scenario with either fight or flight. We all know what it feels like to have adrenaline flush through our system: Our heart starts to race, we can begin to hyperventilate, and we are ready and on edge to respond to danger in a moment's notice. Maybe the first time you remember experiencing an adrenaline flush was as a child when you woke up in the middle of the night and heard that monster under your bed. Or perhaps you remember the more recent time someone leaned on their car horn and alerted you to an impending collision.

Most often, the initial rush of adrenaline is followed by a hormone I like to call its "big brother," *cortisol*. Cortisol helps to support adrenaline and sustain its effects. It rises and lowers at a slower rate than adrenaline. Cortisol also has what we call a "set point." The higher your set point, the more easily you will be triggered for an anxiety-type response to any given incident. A person's set point can increase with repeated exposure to cortisol. A higher set point and the resulting prolonged exposure can ultimately imapct someone's immune, digestive and reproductive systems and other processes in the body; however, your set point can be lowered with ARP, preventing any permanent harm. As you learn and practice the techniques in this book, you will lower your set point.

Here are the direct physiological responses to an increase in adrenaline and cortisol:

~~Symptoms of a Panic Attack~~

Symptoms of Elevated Adrenaline and Cortisol

- Elevated heart rate
- Hyperventilation, difficulty breathing and/or a feeling of choking
- Heavy chest and/or chest pains
- Dry mouth
- Increased physical strength
- A warm, tingly feeling in your extremities (this is due to a redistribution of an oxygen-enriched blood supply to critical areas to help you in fight or flight, i.e., to the muscles in your legs and arms)
- A feeling that you are dying (this is due to your blood being distributed away from non-essential systems, resulting in these systems sending a signal to your brain that they are dying)
- Feeling a loss of control
- Possible nausea and/or dizziness

Most often, we interpret all of these feelings/symptoms as something we have been calling a panic attack. You now know, however, what's going on at a deeper level. These symptoms are very specifically a direct result of elevated levels of adrenaline and cortisol in your body. It is critically important to make this distinction. To end your panic attacks and manage your anxiety, you need to be clear on where to target the tools you are about to learn. In other words, you'll have more success if your objective is to lower these two hormones than if your intention is to try to fight off a panic attack, which has just the opposite effect.

Remember: Your amygdala is on constant alert for any sign that it should respond with fight or flight. The *moment* you even ***think*** about "fighting" off the symptoms of a panic attack (as opposed to thinking about regulating your hormones), *all* the amygdala hears and notices is your intention to "fight"—and quicker than you can blink, it ups the level of cortisol, in return giving you more, and more extreme, symptoms.

In practice, you may have figured this out, because the harder you fight the worse the panic attack feels. So instead of fighting panic attacks, which you may have tried to do all your life, you need to stop the fight and learn to redirect your thinking to the job of regulating your hormones. Put down your weapons and pick up your tools. When dealing with panic and anxiety, you need to think about going to work, not war!

Here then is the second key learning in ending your panic attacks:

Never fight a panic attack!

OK, that is easier said than done. I get it. And, I promise you, by the time you finish reading this book, you will be both prepared and practiced at thinking about regulating your hormones, and not thinking about fighting a panic attack.

Celebratory Anxiety

Wait! What? Celebratory Anxiety? Yes, my friends, it's a real thing!

You adrenaline junkies out there know exactly where I am going next. I have stood in line with friends who are roller-coaster fans as they waited to be willingly and eagerly strapped into a tiny cart that would toss them around at extreme speeds, heights and dizzying spins. Furthermore, they paid to get in this line so they could feel their adrenaline and cortisol soar!

This physiological response of elevated adrenaline and cortisol, which is so good at rescuing you from danger, can also give you a great feeling you might know as a "rush." This elevation is also very good at making you perform certain tasks well.

World-class athletes manage their adrenaline and cortisol

release with precision. Athletes need to hit peak performance in a specific moment that requires an elevated heart rate to move heavily oxygenated blood to critical areas of the body, but not so much that the elevation leads them to panic. This is very similar to how a well-functioning amygdala triggers your stress response when you're walking into that final exam, ensuring your heart is beating a little faster and well-oxygenated blood is supplied to your brain so you can ace that test.

Even children invite adrenaline and elevated cortisol. At the playground you may hear the screams of eager children on the swings: "Daddy, push me higher!"

I'm not a fan of roller coasters, but I do plan on jumping out of a perfectly good plane on my sixtieth birthday. Some of my friends think this idea is proof that I am a bit crazy (I do plan to have a parachute on my back!). But I like to face my fears (it somehow makes me feel like I am still growing up), and I like that anticipatory rush I get all over my body when I am about to do something scary (but ultimately not *too* dangerous). My heart races, my hands sweat, my breathing escalates, I can even feel a bit queasy—oh wait, aren't those the symptoms of anxiety?

Big fat NO my friends!

These symptoms are *best described* as the symptoms of elevated adrenaline and cortisol. And I like them, and I seek them out. This is Celebratory Anxiety, and it is a good thing.

Celebratory Anxiety can be as small as that little rush you feel when you find that perfect dress or widget you needed, and it's the last one and 70 percent off! Or it can be a much bigger feeling, such as when you get a promotion or kiss someone for the first time. With Celebratory Anxiety, the physical response mechanism is the same as less-manageable anxiety, the levels of adrenaline and cortisol simply remain below a point where they feel unpleasant or dangerous.

Knowing that our anxiety can also be fun and helpful is

critical in putting our feelings in perspective. Recognizing Celebratory Anxiety as a degree of the same function that leads us to panic also gives us a chance to pause and evaluate if the physical feeling is warranted, or even chosen. Celebratory Anxiety is a big part of this big ball of feelings we thought we wanted to ditch—but in this case don't. Some of the weight of that big ball is pretty awesome when you stop to think about it. So, stop and think about it!

It is important to really notice the times you experience Celebratory Anxiety. Ask your partner or friends to point out to you moments when they can tell you are ramped up in a good way. By taking note of these moments, we expose ourselves to the positive side of our anxiety response. Like exposure therapy, this helps teach our brains that the physical sensations we associate with anxiety and panic are not always a problem, and can even be desirable.

So, who wants to come with me on my sixtieth birthday and jump out of a plane?

Celebratory Anxiety is that awesome *rush* we feel when doing something fun or when getting a reward.

Now you have the good news about your anxiety: In the right times and at the right levels, elevated cortisol and adrenaline are incredibly helpful, possibly life-saving, or just fun.

These hormones set you up to run and or fight by feeding your muscles with oxygen and sugar rich blood as fuel. When we are in this elevated state we often exhibit increased strength. Lifeguards know to pass a flotation device to someone drowning in panic because their increased super strength can overwhelm the lifeguard. And there are countless stories of how people have saved them selves or other with seemingly super human strength due to these elevated hormones.

And more good news—you can learn to change your thoughts and prevent becoming a victim to those negative, evolutionary bias-based feelings. And ARP can teach you how to change that meltdown, that hot mess, into your superpower! If you keep reading, I promise to show you how.

Neuroplasticity
is the brain's ability to
change and learn.

NEUROPLASTICITY

The 3 keys:
Intention, Repetition & Reward

Chapter Three

WHY THE **ANXIETY RELEASE PROTOCOL** (ARP) WORKS

Getting To Know Your Brain

I am old enough to have witnessed many scientific "facts" change as science and psychology developed over the decades through practice and research. When I went to school, I was taught that the brain is not a very flexible organ, and that, "in fact," by the time we reach our early- to mid-twenties, it is pretty much done growing and changing. I learned that we're pretty much stuck with what we've developed by that point, lending some scientific credibility to the old saying, "You cannot teach an old dog new tricks."

This "fact" was *wrong*. We now understand the brain to have a nature that we describe as "plastic." (I had some pretty self-assured professors who knew they were right about this—another good example of why it's better to be curious than right!) Your brain can be trained, intentionally and otherwise, to rewire its internal connections. This can occur as either a natural process or a process enhanced through learning and training. The characteristic of our brains that allows it to change is called *neuroplasticity*.

Neuroplasticity: How to Change Your Brain

Lars was a bright, 17-year-old honour student who loved football. Considering how much time he invested in his beloved sport, it was amazing that he actually had the time to be an honour student! If Lars wasn't on the field, he was watching the game from the sidelines, working hard at practice with his coach, teaching younger students to play or was on his mobile playing football apps. Lars was very good at the game, and he always wanted to be better. He was extremely focused and committed.

One spring, Lars's plate started to overflow: A sibling was facing health challenges that required the time and care of the entire family; his grandfather, whom he loved dearly, became terminally ill and was considering assisted suicide; and while juggling all of this, plus football and school, Lars was bouncing between two families, since his parents were divorced and both remarried. Everyone knew Lars to be a great student who could handle it all. But Lars was 17, and no matter how together people thought he could keep it, we all have our breaking point.

In the year leading up to that time, Lars had started to experience what he called "red alerts." He would be sitting in class, and suddenly his heart would begin to pound out of his chest and his face would turn beet red. He would just know that everyone was looking at him and it would always seem to him that the only option was to bolt out of the classroom and get himself somewhere else—*anywhere* else. Yet beating those hasty retreats never seemed to help. His panic attacks would get worse no matter where he was, and they terrified and embarrassed him. With life having put so much responsibility on his young plate, Lars would fight hard to do everything, *anything*, to make these attacks stop.

He was sent to the school psychologist who taught him breathing exercises and began a Cognitive Behavioural Therapy (CBT) program with him. She told him he needed to start meditating. When he suffered an attack, the school gave him a quiet space to recover. It was all well intentioned, but no one told Lars that very crucial point (which you now know): *Never fight a panic attack!* So the attacks continued, growing worse and more frequent, until his mother found my office and brought her willing-but-exhausted son in to talk.

And Lars loved to talk, mostly about football! I knew very little about the game, and he was more than ready to teach me. So I taught Lars about anxiety and panic attacks, and he told me all I could learn about football (without actually playing it). We talked about his game and his coach, and how he made the most out of his practices.

As it turned out, Lars was a left-footed kicker. Apparently, in football we have a tendency to use and perfect our kick with only one foot, just like we have a dominant hand with which we write and do other things. Lars was a rare left-footed kicker. He could drive a football with his left foot from one end of the field to the other with deadly accuracy.

I said to him, "Lars, answer me this: If I hosted a reality TV show and the deal was that I would give you thirty days to show up on set, and with a single try kick a football from half-way down the field through the goal posts, with your *right* foot, could you? And here's the kicker: If you make it on the first shot, you win a million bucks."

Lars smiled and quickly checked in to see whether my proposal was hypothetical or not. "Sadly," I said, "it is hypothetical. But it is a very real and important question. So could you?"

Lars instantly responded: "Yeah, I could nail that in thirty days."

I said, "So Lars, what would you have to do in the next thirty days to make sure you nailed it and made your million bucks?"

"Practice, Todd, practice," he said. "I would practice like crazy. My buds and I would *live* on that field and my coach would be all over it too!"

"So you would intentionally hit the field 24/7, practice like a world class athlete, and your coach would back you up with some pretty strong support?"

"Absolutely," Lars responded.

And with that conversation, Lars and I had unpacked the most important three things you need to know about neuroplasticity.

Lars would *intentionally* hit the practice field, *repeatedly* kick the football with this right foot, and surround himself with buddies and coaches that would encourage his success, in turn giving him a solid feeling of *reward*. When these three elements are in place, neuroplastic change most successfully occurs.

The 3 key elements of neuroplastic change are:
Intention, Repetition and Reward

(Please say that out loud right now! And it is best to repeat it a few times!)

You, just by reading this book, are actually making an *Intentional* decision to participate in a process that creates internal change. And congratulations for that investment in *Repetition* just a moment ago—it makes a difference to your ability to end panic attacks and manage anxiety. Well done. Did you notice that congratulatory *Reward* I slipped in there? Notice the feeling of Reward you may be experiencing at this moment. That's the powerful triumvirate: *Intention, Repetition* and *Reward.*

You will notice throughout reading this book and going through the ARP that every step of the solution to ending your panic attacks and managing your anxiety is structured with Intention, Repetition and Reward. No matter what kind of change you are trying to make in your life, any plan or strategy that is going to implement change for the long term will require you to rewire your brain, and to do that you will need to implement change with Intention, Repetition and Reward (OK, that's the fourth time we've repeated it! Do you see what we're doing here? ;)).

The only thing in this world we truly have complete control over is what we think.

Why are these three components of implementing neuronal change so necessary? Their value is recognized by many therapists, and to varying degrees these three elements have been built into different therapeutic modalities, such as Cognitive Behavioural Therapy, Exposure Therapy and Hypnotherapy. There is a saying in the neuroplasticity world: "The neurons that fire together wire together." (Neurons are cellular networks in your brain that transport information with both chemicals and electrical signals.)

Prior to his million-dollar offer, when Lars was about to kick a football, the neurons that held his intent would automatically transport the signal to the series of motor neurons that would in turn make him kick the ball with his left foot. Lars had intentionally kicked a ball with great success with his left foot possibly millions of times, so this neuronal pathway was very well wired together. When he had a reason to kick with his right foot, he needed to develop a new neuronal pathway in order to kick the ball effectively, and that, as you know by now, begins with the first of the three elements of neuronal change.

Intention

Intention is your set-up for neuronal change. If Lars undertook my challenge (and I had a million dollars to spare on a bet!), and he hit the football field to practice, he would be doing so with a very clear Intention: He was going to learn to kick the football with his right foot. He then, subsequently, focused his thoughts and physical resources on preparing to kick the football in a way his brain would have found awkward and uncomfortable. If he failed to hold his Intention, the neurons that had fired together so many times, and were now wired together, would push him instinctively back to using his left foot. This is what people mean by "force of habit."

To kick the ball effectively with his right foot, the star football player had to firmly maintain his Intention throughout the kick, as strange as it felt. And then he had to do it again, and again and again...

Real change is *always* uncomfortable! Embrace uncomfortable, it is the harbinger of change!

Repetition

We all know how this works: Pretty much any skill you have learned, you have done so with practice. In your brain, it is this Repetition that continually fires the neurons that give you the outcome you desire. In Lars's case, it was getting out on that field, day after day, and kicking the football over and over again with his right foot instead of his dominant left foot. And as you now know, the neurons that *fire* together *wire* together. The more he kicked that ball with his right foot, the more natural it felt and the more consistently the ball flew as far as it would if he'd kicked it with his left.

Reward

The final stage in creating neuronal change is incredibly important. Taking notice of, and investing in, the pleasure you get from the outcome of a change, or even just the sense of Reward you get from showing up and practicing, counts. Your brain's ability to get you to repeat an action that brings you pleasure is astonishing.

What happens in the brain when you experience pleasure is complicated: It involves a number of regions, hormones and signals. The neurotransmitter called dopamine is released into your nucleus accumbens (a lower part of your brain) and your hippocampus (a small organ in the middle of your brain); your amygdala then stores information (memories) about what is happening. This network gives you a powerful shortcut to know how to repeat the necessary actions in order to get the same pleasurable feeling again. (OK, that was really geeky for everyone except you science majors. Don't worry, these details aren't really necessary for the ARP to work; they were just a nice little bonus for us nerdy folks!)

Much of what we have learned about how the brain's pleasure centre operates comes from addiction research. If you are familiar with addiction, you may have witnessed firsthand how someone who becomes addicted, be it to alcohol, drugs or a particular behaviour such as watching Internet pornography, can very quickly replace their usual, healthy behaviour with behaviour that feeds the addiction. In some unfortunate situations, individuals lose everything in their lives in their quest to continue abusing a particular substance. This illustrates how plastic our brains are and how powerful the brain's pleasure centre is in getting us to repeat behaviour, even when the new behavior is a destructive one.

The good news is the urge to repeat actions that light up the reward centre of the brain can be harnessed to achieve positive outcomes as effectively as it can be used to achieve negative outcomes like addiction. In ARP—the solution to end your panic attacks and transform your anxiety—you are going to use this capacity to encourage a positive outcome in your life. You are going to intentionally notice, with Reward, the pleasure that a particular action brings you. You are going to intentionally do your best to encourage your brain to lay down a neural network to get you intuitively repeating desired processes or actions.

Understanding Neuroplastic Change

Imagine that you live in a farmhouse across a cornfield from your best friend. Over the years, you have acquired the habit of waking up, grabbing your trusty dog named Doogle and heading out across the cornfield to your friend's house to share morning coffee. Although it's a good 20-minute walk through corn stalks that tower high above your head, you have done the morning walk so many times that you could likely do it blindfolded.

But we all have mornings when things don't go as they should, and on this morning good old Doogle hears something off the beaten path and, despite your pre-caffeinated protests, bolts out of sight. Being the good dog-daddy or -mommy that you are, you take off after Doogle. As you run you are hit in the face by corn stalks and you stumble over ruts in the soil and really have no idea where you are going, aside from following the sound of Doogle's bark.

Eventually you catch up, and whatever Doogle was chasing is long gone. Doogle is patiently waiting beside a small stream you have never noticed before, as it is well off your usual path. You grab Doogle and the two of you follow the stream until it eventually leads you to your friend's house. As it turns out, once you realize you aren't terribly lost you notice that following the stream makes for an enjoyable walk.

The following morning, you think it might be worth taking the stream route again. You enter the cornfield at your usual point, carefully looking for where you deviated from your path the morning before. You spot a few broken stalks, then look for more until, with attention and effort, you find the stream again. It isn't an easy path to find, and the tight rows of corn and then the uneven ground along the stream can be pretty uncomfortable in spots, but eventually you make your way to your friend's house.

The new route is interesting enough that over the next few days and weeks you choose this alternative path again and again and are rewarded with a new experience and enjoyable walk. Each day the path becomes easier to find, and within a few weeks it takes very little of your attention to follow this enjoyable new route to your friend's for morning coffee.

Neuroplastic change is very much like this story. The paths through the cornfield are like neuronal pathways. When they are well used and you are practiced in following them, you don't have to pay much attention to finding your way or performing a task or a thought. However, when you choose a *new* path, it's not easy to see it at first, it's uncomfortable to travel and it can take a fair bit of Intention and Repetition to master. But the Rewards of your progress on this new route drive you to keep trying, despite the discomfort.

Here is a good place to notice that being uncomfortable is a good thing. It is a sign of *change*. If you are uncomfortable because of a new chosen path, *embrace* the feeling; it is the sign that the change is happening. After all, you are going to feel uncomfortable only until you don't, and that is when you have solidly wired those new neurons together to create a new you.

Being uncomfortable is the harbinger of change!

If you want to fire a new series of neuronal pathways, you really need to pay attention (Intention), and it's likely to be difficult and uncomfortable at first. If you persist in making the new choice over and over (Repetition), you will find over time that the new pathway that provided an enjoyable walk by the stream (Reward) will become as easy to find as the old.

Let's use this story again to illustrate one more characteristic of neuroplastic change: Eventually the corn stalks on the original path will grow back. The old path will become less and less inviting as it becomes more difficult to navigate. After quite some time, years perhaps, with a little effort, you might be able to find the original path again, but that too would require starting the neuroplastic change process of Intention and Repetition.

Neuroplasticity, or the ability to rewire your brain, is the key reason you have the ability to overcome panic attacks and manage your anxiety. The incredible capacity to use Intention, Repetition and Reward to become the person you *choose* to be is nothing less than amazing. These are the keys to transforming your anxiety into your superpower!

As you learn the techniques in this book, you are not only changing how you experience your world, you are actually changing your brain. Beginning today, you are learning how to make intentional choices about how you want that change to look. And just like our football player Lars, who didn't get his million dollars but did learn the implications of retraining himself to kick the ball with his non-dominant foot, you now know that it's possible to change from being someone who experiences spiking cortisol in the form of panic attacks and is at the mercy of their anxiety to someone who is panic attack-free and easily transforms their anxiety.

Fuel a diesel engine with gas,
the engine will fail.

Fuel your brain with junk,
your brain will fail.

FOOD IS FUEL

Chapter Four

PREPARING YOUR BRAIN FOR CHANGE: FOUR KEY BUILDING BLOCKS FOR A HEALTHY BRAIN

Brain Fuel

Many years ago, I dated a very gifted figure skater who went on to win multiple Olympic medals. As I was a young man busy with life and building a career, many of the opportunities the relationship might have afforded were lost on me. One of those opportunities I most often saw as a problem. At the time, I associated food with pleasure, not fuel. For Olympians, as much as they may enjoy eating, food's most valuable and essential role is fueling their bodies (including their brains). I can't tell you how many times I rolled my eyes at a dinner carefully crafted to provide the necessary elements and nutrition for peak performance. Thoughtlessly, I would shrug and chow down on my burger and fries with extra mayo.

I love food. Over the years, my palate has expanded and matured. I'm what we now call a "foodie." I also love to cook. My friends often show up at my door unannounced around dinnertime, and this has led me to the conclusion I am a pretty darn good in the kitchen. I'm one of those guys who finds cooking relaxing and rewarding. For me, it falls somewhere between an art and a science. I am eager to do copious amounts of research to figure out why a soufflé rises, or why a roast can emerge from an oven crusty on the outside and moist and tender on the inside. And I consider butter a food of the gods!

What I didn't pay much attention to until the last few years is the science of how food impacts not just our bodies, but our brains. I confess I was surprised when a noted psychologist and neuroscientist presented me with piles of clinical research about how powerfully and directly certain foods and nutrients could encourage neuronal growth and plasticity, and how others could actually make the pathways in our brain brittle and difficult to change, and even lead to memory loss. Much of this research looked at detailed brain scans of people with varied, and often extreme, diets. The scans of those who consumed large amounts of sugar and simple carbohydrates (white flour, pasta... all that comfort-food stuff) showed alarming images. They revealed, in detailed Technicolor, regions of their brains that were limited in function; plaque, which impedes memory and learning, had formed in critical regions of their learning and memory centres. What I was looking at were brains that were breaking down, becoming brittle and losing function. And the two biggest culprits were sugar and carbohydrates.

We all know how quickly foods like sugar can influence our behaviour and thoughts. The managers of the day-care centre at my ski club certainly do. There hangs a sign: "Children not picked up by closing time will be given chocolate-covered espresso beans and a free puppy!" Every parent knows that sugar makes their kid bounce off the walls in a matter of minutes. Not surprisingly, everyone was on time at the end of the ski day to collect their little ones!

Of course, it's not just kids who react badly to eating too much of the wrong foods. How much do you know about your own post-lunch carb crash? It can be almost impossible to stay awake after eating a large amount of carbohydrates. A complex process that includes your sugar levels makes you incredibly tired and moves your brain into sleep mode. Whether it is a sugar rush or a carb crash, these symptoms represent some serious physical changes happening in your brain. Many of these changes can encourage panic and anxiety and increase your cortisol set point.

It is unfortunate, but many of us give more attention to the fuel we put into our cars than the fuel we put into our bodies. It would never even occur to us to top up our diesel-engine car with gasoline, or vice versa.

If you want to end your panic attacks and manage your anxiety, you need to ensure that your brain has the right fuel for the job.

The human body (including our brain) functions best if we fuel it constantly. In an ideal world, we would graze all day and night, consuming small amounts of food at least every two hours. In doing so, our sugar levels would remain balanced and our body would not be triggered to store fats. Yet we have to sleep, and for the average human that includes 7-8 hours of solid rest. Interestingly, sleep provides a period of fasting, several continual hours without eating. Fasting is known to improve brain function. Your mom was right: Get your sleep, and breakfast (or "breaking fast") really *is* the most important meal of the day.

What happens when you skip breakfast?

- Decreased problem solving skills
- Decreased working memory
- Decreased attention
- Decreased concentration
- Decreased energy
- Increased mood swings
- Increased feeling of depression
- Increased reactions to stress
- Increased anxiety
- Increased propensity for panic attacks

We all know that crash or fad diets don't work as long-term solutions; if they produce any benefits, they often don't last. So take a deep breath here: My experience with many, many clients has taught me that nutrition, although critical, does not need to include any extreme diet measures.

What's most important is to know *what is good for your brain* and *what is not*, and to eat accordingly. Mashed potatoes with your Thanksgiving turkey will not kill you; it's just that you'll likely sleep through the washing up! Take note of the following foods and nutrients that our brilliant researchers have figured out either help or hurt your brain, and do your best to minimize the bad stuff and maximize the good stuff. The best source of any nutrient is fresh, organic food. However, since this is not always an option, eat as fresh and healthy as you can, and use quality supplements to fill in your nutritional gaps.

Quit worrying about sticking to a complicated or long-term diet. Do not be concerned about what you're going to eat except for what you're going to pick up *in this moment*. Stay present. Work this change one mouthful and one meal at a time.

An easy way to avoid overeating while consuming a good

balance of foods is to ensure at every meal you eat a balanced portion of protein, vegetables and healthy carbohydrates. A ready guide can be based on your hand size. A handful of protein, a handful of good carbohydrates and two handfuls of vegetables. For a lighter meal or snack, just retain these proportions of 1:1:2.

The following table will give you a good idea of what to eat and what to avoid. Copy it and post it in your kitchen as a reminder.

Take this list with you to the grocery store and stock up on the good stuff and avoid the bad stuff.

Keep in mind that there are guidelines for daily requirements (and limits) of most food and nutrients. Government agencies publish guidelines, and you can glean some useful insight from dietitians, and professional physical trainers and athletes who understand that food is really fuel for the brain and body.

The Good Stuff and the Bad Stuff

The Good Stuff

- Amino Acids
  - Lean red meat, poultry, seafood, pork, eggs & dairy, quinoa, tofu
- Omega-3s and 6s
  - Fatty fishes like salmon, tuna and halibut
  - Oils: flaxseed, hemp, soybean, canola and walnut
  - Soy and tofu
  - Green leafy vegetables
  - Venison and buffalo
  - Some eggs are enhanced with omega 3s
- Legumes
  - Lentils, chickpeas, beans
- Essential Fatty Acids (EFAs)
- Polyphenols
  - Green tea
  - Apples
  - Soy
  - Blueberries, elderberries and cherries
- Antioxidants from Phytonutrients
  - Blueberries, blackberries, strawberries, raspberries and plums
  - Spinach
- Good Carbohydrates (unprocessed)
  - Buckwheat
  - Slow cooked, steel-cut oatmeal
  - Millet
  - Cream of wheat
  - Seed breads
- Sage, oregano, thyme and other herbs and spices
- Vitamin D
- Small, regular meals

The Bad Stuff

There are 3 primary things to look out for an avoid:

1. SUGAR
   (The refined types, like white sugar, are the unhealthiest)

2. REFINED CARBOHYDRATES
   (When in excess and not balanced with protein)
   - Refined flours often found in pasta and other dishes and products like white bread and cereals

3. TRANS-FATTY ACIDS ALSO KNOWN AS UNSATURATED FATS (Seriously bad news!)
   - Spot them on the label as 'Partially Hydrogenated Oils'
   - An 'artificial' fat made by adding hydrogen to oil often added to make a food more solid

     These are absorbed directly into the body and brain blocking the body's ability to make its own EFAs, can alter neurotransmitters such as dopamine (the feel-good hormone), negatively impact the brain's blood supply, increase your bad cholesterol while decreasing your good cholesterol, build plaque in your blood vessels reducing oxygen to your brain, cause excessive body fat.

Here are a few classic foods where you will encounter this 'Bad Stuff'

Cookies, donuts, potato chips, candy, mayonnaise, vegetable shortening, crackers, cake, deep-fried foods, cheese puffs, margarine, fast food, pre-made often frozen products like corn dogs, breakfast sandwiches and pastries, and ready-to-bake rolls and confections.

A final note:

Avoid large, irregular and poorly proportioned meals, which can cause spikes in your sugar, triggering fat storage in your body and other negative outcomes

Keep Your Brain Lubricated

Our bodies are almost 65 percent water. Water plays a role in every function of the body and brain. Staying hydrated is so important, I could write an entire book on why.

Adults should aim to drink at least 2.2 litres, or 9 cups, of water per day (men typically require slightly more than women: 3 litres or 12 cups). Hot days or days of heavy exercise will, of course, require higher consumption.

Water is absolutely critical to your brain function. It also:

- Controls your body temperature
- Aids digestion
- Carries nutrients around your body and to your brain
- Lubricates and cushions organs and joints
- Gets rid of waste and helps you detoxify
- Keeps your bowels regular.

A lack of water can severely impede your brain function and, as a result, make it easier for your body to default to anxiety responses.

Some of the symptoms of dehydration include:

- Being thirsty
- Dry lips and mouth
- Flushed skin
- Fatigue
- Irritability
- Headache and dizziness
- Fainting
- Low blood pressure
- Increased heart rate
- Dark, strong smelling urine.

Severe dehydration can result in:

- Blue lips
- Blotchy skin
- Confusion
- Lack of energy
- Cold hands and feet
- Rapid breathing
- High fever
- Unconsciousness.

I encourage you to drink water regularly and often. Begin your day right. Start your morning with a large glass of water to rehydrate after your sleep. I fill a one-litre jug and drink it while I am getting ready for work in the morning.

Until consuming lots of water on a regular basis becomes a habit, carry a water bottle with you at all times. Keep it within easy reach and view. Think of a drink of water as a kick-start to any performance: a task at work, a walk, reading or housework. And please, don't buy boxes of plastic bottles; think *green*. There are reusable water bottles on the market that have built-in filters, and you can personalize them. Make your reusable water bottle your "thing"!

Whatever the activity, always start with a drink of water. Think of it as lubrication for your brain. That well-balanced breakfast is a good start to your day, but drink lots of water and you'll start your day even better. Not only will your mom be proud, your brain will thank you.

Recharge for Peak Performance

> *"It is a common experience that a problem difficult at night is resolved in the morning after the committee of sleep has worked on it."*
>
> *– John Steinbeck*

There is a darn good neurological reason to back Mr. Steinbeck on this one. It is during sleep that we not only recharge most of the systems in our body, but it is also believed that the mind solves lingering problems and makes sense of our day, consolidating experiences, sensations and events into coherent and manageable memories. If we fail to do this recharge and don't process the events of the day, we are *primed* for panic attacks and high levels of anxiety.

You might be sighing in despair as you read this section: *Sleep? With anxiety? And if by some miracle I do doze off, I only wake up with my heart beating out of my chest in the midst of a panic attack!* This is a common occurrence if your cortisol set point has been pushed too high. Remember: These symptoms are always best described as the symptoms of excess adrenaline and cortisol. Many of my clients experience sleep loss as an unpleasant side effect of a high cortisol set point.

You can find rest and rejuvenation in your sleep by committing to some basic sleep hygiene regimens. Like most activities, sleep can be a learned habit. So remember, Intention, Repetition and Reward come into play here, too.

Here is a checklist to help you develop a sleep regimen that can minimize the impact of anxiety on getting a proper night's rest:

1. Create a dedicated sleeping place.

Even if you do not have the luxury of a dedicated bedroom, carve out a space that you use only for sleep. Get a comfortable mattress, comfy sheets and a pillow designed for your sleeping position (are you a side sleeper or a back sleeper, for instance). Use your bed only to sleep, not as a place to read or do homework. (OK, good sex is the one exception here!)

- Make certain a comfortable temperature and humidity is maintained all night.

- Soundproof the area. If you cannot block out ambient sounds, get comfortable earplugs and a white-noise generator to mask them. White noise is a hissing sound that encompasses a full range of audible frequencies that somewhat block out background sounds.
- Block out light. If you cannot get the room dark, use a soft, comfortable blindfold.

2. Start preparing to sleep early.

Even when you get enough practice at getting a good sleep, set up a positive expectation for the upcoming quiet time. Being still and resting may not be as good as sleep, but it beats the heck out of running around stressing before bed.

Sleeping well takes some planning. Getting as much natural light as you can during the day is very important in helping your body adopt a healthy sleeping rhythm. If you live in a cold climate with dark winters, make certain you supplement your diet with Vitamin D, often called the "sun vitamin."

Set a regular bedtime and waking time, and stick to them.

Most adults function ideally on 7-8 hours of sleep.

Make certain you do not eat or drink stimulants in the afternoon or evening. Coffee, caffeinated tea, energy drinks, chocolate, or anything with caffeine or sugar should be altogether avoided in your diet, or at least restricted to morning hours. Alcohol is a tricky substance: It makes you feel like you are sleepy, then causes you to sleep poorly. Don't drink before bed, and if you smoke, avoid smoking before bed. Nicotine is a stimulant, just like alcohol and caffeine.

Start getting ready for bed two hours in advance. Dim your lights and turn off the music, or switch it to something quiet and relaxing. Avoid TVs or any visual electronics. The blue light from screens can stimulate your brain in a way very unhelpful before bed. So yes, even turn off that phone for the night. Right off! The world will still be there in the morning.

Also:

- Crawl into snuggly pajamas or something *really* comfortable.
- A small, light snack such as cheese and a few crackers with warm milk (not chocolate) or chamomile tea can be helpful. Warm water is easier on the stomach and absorbs quicker than cold water into your system. I like to sip a small quantity of plain, filtered, hot water as I get ready for bed as part of my three litres each day.
- Consider a relaxing hot bath. (You deserve it for working so hard reading and implementing what's in this book!)

Create a ritual around these activities to get ready for bedtime that includes the final pieces in your "Daily 5" that you will learn about a bit later in this book. Because sleep is a learned skill. Just like anything else, we need to approach it Intentionally, repeating the steps that lead us towards our goal, and celebrating our efforts and victories, however small.

Later you will learn some very practical techniques to lower your cortisol and calm your mind. It is wise to integrate these new skills into your preparation ritual for sleep.

Get Moving!

Honest confession: I do not like to exercise.

I've tried everything from hiring eager trainers to taking up active sports in the hopes of getting hooked.

Nope. Not my thing.

I deeply admire the work of the great creator when she designed the sloth. That fuzzy beast hits a top speed of three metres per minute, and that's upside down in a tree! The sloth has a very slow metabolism, and as a result this lazy beast does just fine with nothing we'd consider exercise.

But we humans, we need to *move*. Our metabolism is not designed to be stationary, but to perform best when pushed a bit. The saying "Use it or lose it" very much applies when it comes to our body.

It is not just your mobility and longevity that depend on exercise; your brain needs the support of your body and all of its systems in order to perform well. Critically, your heart pumps oxygen and nutrient-rich blood to your brain, and this is the very fuel that makes your brain function well. Neglect any link in the system, and you mess with your brain (making it more susceptible to unmanageable anxiety).

The idea here is to *get active*. Join a gym or play a recreational sport like squash or tennis. Keep in mind that just about *anything* can become habit, and even an addiction, if you keep at it long enough, exercise included. And if you just can't wrap your ahead around these high-intensity activities, then at least find *some* way to get moving.

The best I have figured out as a bottom line, should you not be a gym bunny or hooked on an exercise-dependent sport or activity, is this: Get your heart rate escalated for at least 20 minutes a day. There are many ways to do this:

- Get off transit a stop early on your way to work or home, and walk briskly the rest of the way.
- Play with your kids in the park and try to keep up.
- Take the dog for a brisk walk.
- Take the stairs or get off the elevator a floor (or four!) early.
- Invite your clients or colleagues to meetings that take place while out walking. It's not surprising that better ideas seem to spring forth when your brain is getting a steady supply of well-oxygenated blood.
- Go swimming.
- Join a square-dance group or take your other half to swing classes (this can make a fun first date too!).

- Start walking or biking to work.
- Become an explorer: Check out local parks and trails.

Piles of options are at your disposal whether you live in a city or the country. Get creative and get busy, and moving. Just 20 minutes a day will make a huge difference to your state of mind.

These four key components—food, water, sleep and exercise—underpin a healthy life and a healthy brain.

Post-Traumatic Stress Disorder and Anxiety

Post-Traumatic Stress Disorder (PTSD) is a condition in which people who have experienced a traumatic event, such as assault, find themselves suffering a number of unpleasant physical and mental symptoms long after the event has passed. One of the many symptoms is unmanageable anxiety, frequent panic attacks and a limited ability to sleep, or bad sleep. PTSD is one of the frequent reasons my clients come to me to end panic attacks and learn to manage their anxiety.

Because anxiety and panic attacks are all too often connected to PTSD, let's take a minute to understand the connection and its relationship to the ARP.

It is understood that PTSD symptoms can largely be attributed to a lack of subconscious processing during sleep. Researchers are beginning to understand that during REM (Rapid Eye Movement) sleep, we seem to gather all the bits and pieces of the events of our day, and we somehow consolidate them into a comprehensive memory with a beginning, middle and an end. Our now-orderly memories of the day are then filed away for future retrieval in our hippocampus.

In the case of any event, including a potentially traumatic event, we take the information into our brain through our senses. There are sounds, smells, tastes, feelings and of course the sights we see. These pieces of information are all fragments of a complete picture or story, and if left scattered about the brain—and not consolidated into a complete picture during sleep—they can seem puzzling or even frightening when retrieved.

If you suffer from PTSD, you know that panic attacks and high-level anxiety are often part of the package. You might experience random triggers—say a particular sound or smell—that were associated with the event that was part of the trauma. The brain of a PTSD survivour is unable to connect the dots back to the memory in that moment. The brain recognizes imminent danger without understanding why, and the amygdala instantly releases adrenaline followed by cortisol.

It is important if you believe you have PTSD or think that in some way your panic attacks or high anxiety levels are connected to a past traumatic event that you seek out a trauma therapist, ideally one who practices EMDR (Eye Movement Desensitization and Reprocessing) therapy. This particular therapy seeks to replicate the brain activity normally found in REM sleep to help desensitize your triggers by folding them into the complete memory in the same way healthy sleep does. EMDR is often a very helpful therapeutic modality in combination with other forms of treatment.

Having PTSD does not stop the techniques in this book from alleviating the symptoms of high cortisol and adrenaline in your system. A good therapist will teach many of the things you will learn in this book to help you alleviate PTSD symptoms. A good therapist will also help you get to the bottom of why your brain is behaving the way it is at this point in your life, and in unpacking that understanding they can help you prevent your symptoms from returning.

Next: If you are going to rewire your brain to end your panic attacks and learn how to transform your anxiety into your superpower, you need to be working with the best tools and materials, and under the most ideal circumstances you can create. Sleep is critical to our ability to function well, learn these techniques and allow your brain to intentionally build new circuitry for the better. Any engineer will tell you that when you construct a house or a bridge, if you want it to function well and last long, you need to set it on a firm foundation and construct it out of quality materials. Your brain is no different.

You are the engineer here making the calls. This book will give you the best tools possible, but you need to show up with the rest. Let's start rebuilding your panic attack-free brain with the best materials and resources we can muster!

THE ART OF MANAGING STRESS

is in your capacity to understand your brain's wiring.

Capitalize on it

FOR GOOD.

Chapter Five

THE PATH OF LEAST RESISTANCE

Homer Simpson is really an interesting character. If you haven't heard of him before, Homer is the central character in an American cartoon called *The Simpsons*. Homer is a family man. He has an adoring wife and three messy kids, and is a beer-drinking, fun-loving, poorly educated, well-meaning fellow who has the responsibility of working in the control centre of the local nuclear power plant.

Homer also lives in my brain.

More precisely, I've discovered that he has taken up residence in my fight-or-flight center: the amygdala.

The best I can figure is that Homer has lived there since I was born. I really can't complain too much about this meddling fellow, because I managed to survive decades with his hands on the controls that release my adrenaline and cortisol. To his credit, he's done a pretty darn good job of keeping me safe by getting me ready to run out of the way of honking cars and having me avoid scary back alleys.

However, at one point in my life, Homer somehow decided to start working far too hard and way too many hours. It appeared the simplest things would have him flushing my system with adrenaline and cortisol. And since you now understand the symptoms of having high levels of these hormones in your system, you can imagine that my world wasn't too enjoyable.

My stress levels, anxiety and even the occasional panic attack were off the charts, and this was totally unacceptable to me. So when facing a panic attack, my gut reaction was to fight back. I was prepared to do anything to fight off the symptoms. Therapists, psychotherapists and psychologists told me I had all sorts of psychological problems. They named things like Generalized Anxiety Disorder and gave me exercises to fight back with Cognitive Behavioural Therapy homework, meditation homework, and a wide variety of other tools and therapeutic modalities that seemed to help but never solved my problem. I was never able to win the fight against Homer. The psychiatrist would reach for the prescription pad and encourage me to take drugs that would either cover up the symptoms or mess with my brain chemistry. Apparently, they thought I was broken.

I wasn't so sure. But I knew was at my wits' end; I was sick and tired of being sick and tired. The littlest thing would make Homer flush my system with adrenaline and cortisol in a moment's notice.

So I gave up on all the experts and I started to do my own research. I found *tons* of books, research articles and studies on anxiety and panic attacks. I've always loved being an academic, so I dove into the literature and poured through the volumes of materials. In the eyes of my colleagues and even my college at the time, I was becoming a bit of a specialist, or maybe even an expert.

But the truth was, I really didn't know *the answer*. I was

pretty darn good at practicing and even teaching the various modalities that helped. But somehow, no matter how hard I fought with Homer, he just kept overworking.

Here is how I discovered the key to ending my panic attacks.

I love my bed. I really love to sleep. And somehow, Homer's over-activity had reached the point that in the midst of a lovely, warm, cuddly sleep, he would flood me with hormones, and I would wake up and sit bolt upright on the verge of a panic attack. The first time this happened, it was so startling I didn't quite know what to think. The second time it happened I was pissed off! I mean, really, *really* angry.

There are two things in this world everyone who knows me knows not to mess with: my puppy and my sleep. Mess with either and I'm likely to hit a level of crazy that can make one's nightmares seem like a happy place!

Angry and frustrated, on night two of being so rudely awoken, I actually yelled out loud, "What the hell do you want?!" And much to my pleasant surprise, Homer backed down. I could actually feel the adrenaline and cortisol levels dropping in my body! As I sat in my bed realizing how quickly the symptoms were receding, I said, "Thank you," at that point to no one and nothing in particular, just a general "thank you" out to the universe. And my symptoms continued to recede. (As a man always interested in self-development and personal growth, and later as a therapist, I learned the value of being grateful and expressing my gratitude. Gratitude Therapy might be one of the most powerful modalities there is to treat almost any mental disorder. We will discuss this more a little later on in the book.)

So now feeling a bit better, and in complete exasperation, I let out a rather pathetic sounding plea: "What do you want?" Apparently Homer knew he had my attention, and when I expressed gratitude, and looked around my room and knew

I was safe (there were no monsters under my bed that night), he no longer felt the need to get me ready to run or fight.

And as I sat there in gratitude and amazement, it finally hit me. My amygdala, whom I would soon name Homer (I'll explain why shortly), really just wanted two things:

1. My attention—Homer was concerned I was in danger (for some unknown reason) and wanted to make sure I knew about it.
2. My cooperation—Homer wanted me to figure out how to best protect myself from this potential danger.

And just like that, I discovered THE MOST IMPORTANT THING YOU NEED TO KNOW TO END YOUR PANIC ATTACKS AND TRANSFORM YOUR ANXIETY INTO YOUR SUPERPOWER. In case you don't remember it from when we met Lars, the high-school football star, I'll say it again:

NEVER FIGHT A PANIC ATTACK!

The moment you try to fight a panic attack, whether it is with CBT or breathing exercises, or any other way, all Homer hears is your mind gearing up to fight the experience, and Homer, the simple guy he is, floods you with more adrenaline and cortisol. You fight harder, and he releases more hormones, and the war escalates.

And up to that very moment, every professional had been telling me I could "fight" off the feelings if I just used all of the great tools they gave me. Yet here I was, sitting up in bed with my heart pounding.

So, in the wee hours of that morning, a unique plan was hatched. I was done fighting. Like a good parent caring for a screaming, petulant child, I was ready to be compassionate, aware, patient and supportive. I named the guy in my head Homer that night. It was pretty clear that if I gave Homer what he wanted, he was willing to back off. And after all, all he wanted was my attention and to protect me.

Before you close this book and start screaming, "What the hell do you want?" to your anxiety (this is actually *not* a good idea), please know that this discovery precipitated the technique that over 98 percent of my clients find very effective.

It's not tricky, and it's wildly successful.

Are you ready?

Anthropomorphization

Anthropomorphization is a big word that simply means *to attribute human form or traits to things that are not human.* Me calling my amygdala control center "Homer" is an example. In clinical therapeutic speak, it is not unlike the practice of *Externalization* used in *Narrative* and other forms of therapy. Externalization is a process that encourages you to talk about an event in which you were involved, or a feeling you have, in the third person. It helps us separate ourselves from a perceived character trait—perhaps anger. Instead of saying, "I am an angry person," we can reframe the anger and say, "When that happens, the angry part of in my brain shows up, and I want to find a different part to respond next time." Since this language clarifies that it was not all of you or all of your brain that reacted a certain way, it makes sense you could access a different part for a different response.

Since we want to produce a different response to our triggers or the things that seem to cause us anxiety or panic, when we name our control release centre we are able to stop perceiving ourselves as a person with anxiety or panic. Instead, *we are a person who has yet to figure out how to get along with the character making the decisions in our control centre*. So there you have it: There is most likely nothing wrong with you—you just have yet to learn how to get along with your Homer! Remember: Ending panic attacks and managing anxiety is simply a learned skill.

Ending panic attacks and managing anxiety is a learned skill.

So go ahead: Name your amygdala. And since you need to get along with this character, don't name him or her after your arch enemy or your ex's new partner! Pick or create a name that you can work with. Cartoon characters seem to be a favourite of my clients. Every day I get to chat with amygdalas named Stewie, Bugs, Annie, Baloo, Pumbaa, Shrek and the occasional Scooby.

For easy reference, as I share with you the keys to ending your panic attacks and transforming your anxiety, I am going to keep referring to my amygdala as Homer, but you are welcome to start thinking of your own by the name of your choice.

Let's get this relationship started!

If you have been experiencing panic attacks and elevated anxiety for quite some time, you are likely aware of how you typically experience them. They can arrive a bit differently for everyone. You may feel the constricted chest or the breathing problems first, or you may be struck with a wave of nausea, tingly hands or a tingly head. But no matter how your body first responds to an impending attack or anxiety, *take note of the initial symptoms.*

You might even know in advance when you are going to be hit with a panic attack or anxiety. Certain events, people, places, things or even thoughts may trigger you. You might do your best to avoid these things, but life sometimes demands you face them, and the anticipation of doing so can be the first sign of an oncoming attack. Whether you can sense the attack in advance or get hit suddenly, you need to start taking note of the first signs of elevated hormones.

Your initial symptoms, or even your initial thoughts of concern, are simply Homer's way of getting your attention.

STEP ONE

The split second you know Homer is showing up, respond with precisely these two sentences:

1. "Homer,* you wanted my attention, you've got it!"
2. "Homer* you want to keep me safe, I am going to help!"
   *Substitute here the name you have chosen.

Don't make up your own sentences. Just memorize these sentences and stick with them! It is ideal to say these sentences out loud, if at all possible. As you know, if you have a panic attack you would attract more attention than saying these few lines would! Do your best to speak in a clear and caring manner, and get yourself to a place that you will be able to work with Homer.

Go back right now and say these sentences out loud a few dozen times. Remember: Intention, Repetition and Reward. You are going to need these sentences on the tip of your tongue as we learn the strategies of ARP.

These sentences work. They are clear, concise and the perfect answer to Homer. Speaking them out loud is the opposite of ignoring Homer or fighting with him. Give him what he wants. After all, he just wants your attention and for you to be safe.

Many clients report back to me that this frontline strategy—once they know all you now know about the brain, neuroplasticity, anxiety and panic—provides them with instant relief. Some say that these sentences alone can reduce the intensity of a panic attack by as much as 80 percent. Now, that is not everyone, but it is a fine testament to the fact we are on the right path here!

Keeping you safe is fundamentally what Homer wants, so let's move on to convincing him that you are indeed safe.

"Homer, you wanted my attention, you've got it!"
"Homer, you want to keep me safe, I am going to help!"

STEP TWO

Once you have acknowledged Homer with the sentences "Homer, you wanted my attention, you've got it! Homer, you want to keep me safe, I am going to help!" you need to quickly move to *Step Two*: engaging Homer's concern that you are not safe.

If possible, find a quiet place to sit down (because talking to yourself out loud is going to work best, but sometimes draws unwanted attention!). Take a look around and try to determine why he thinks you are in danger.

Think of this stage as a safety inspection. Do you know this place? Does anyone look suspicious? Are there any suspicious packages? Is anyone armed? Is the space itself dangerous (like the edge of a mountain cliff)? Answer these questions out loud (if practical) and direct the answers to Homer. Your conversation with Homer might go something like this:

> "Homer, you wanted my attention, you've got it! Homer, you want to keep me safe, I am going to help!
>
> "I just walked into my regular classroom at school and everything looks pretty normal. I don't see any new faces or see anyone looking upset. Nothing

> looks out of place. The teacher looks safe—preoccupied even. No one looks armed, the door is still open, and there is the fire exit at the rear of the room. They ran a fire alarm test last week so that is good. I've got my schoolbag close at hand and even remembered my homework—so no danger there! I see a few friendly faces I have spoken with before. There seem to be more people smiling than not.
>
> "All looks safe to me, but let me tell you what: Let me work with you here, Homer, and keep an eye out in case anything dangerous crops up. In this moment everything seems pretty safe, but I will keep a watch with you."

You have now satisfied the two key things Homer wants:

1. You have clearly given him your attention.
2. You have supported him by doing a safety check of your environment to ensure you are both safe.

So What if Homer Continues to Release Cortisol?

You can't win them all. And after all, Homer is pretty experienced in flooding you with cortisol. But remember:

1. Panic Attacks are uncomfortable, NOT dangerous.
2. Never Fight a Panic Attack.
3. Panic Attacks always end.

Remember the time your child, or someone else's, had a public meltdown? In a last-ditch attempt to get their way that kid threw themselves on the floor, kicking and screaming, as hundreds of passersby watched? If you weren't the child's parent, you likely smiled, nodded and kept going, thanking the universe the kid was not yours. And if they were your kid, you knew the only option was to stand by, make sure they did not hurt themselves and let them burn it out. Fighting with them, like fighting with Homer, would only escalate the drama. So, if after acknowledging Homer and telling him you would help keep him safe, he *still* decides he need to release that cortisol, wait him out while keeping you both safe. It's uncomfortable but not dangerous, and it will end.

While you are waiting, try a little game with him to help reinforce the fact you are paying attention.

It goes like this:

> "Ok, Homer. If you need to release more cortisol, that's ok. I am here and will keep us safe while you do. Would you like to make my hands tingle now, or maybe my feet? Would it help you to escalate my heart rate? Go ahead, it's all going to be ok..."

And wait him out. You will find the panic attack is less intense and shorter than you might be accustomed to.

Homer, as part of your brain, is always looking for the most effective way to do anything. If you continue to acknowledge and support him, he will soon learn not to expend this much energy to achieve his goal. After all, you are now working in alignment with his goal to keep you safe.

There is more to why this strategy works (although satisfying Homer's concerns is unquestionably the biggest part of preventing your panic attack and minimizing your anxiety). Notice that in this conversation with Homer you are intentionally changing your thoughts, and demanding your brain create new thoughts and discard old ones. You are directing your attention away from the FEAR-based thoughts and creating thoughts that make you present and keep you in the moment. In fact, you are changing your thoughts by *choice*. This ability is a learned skill, and some might even say it is a primary goal of *Mindful Meditation*.

Mindful Meditation is the art and skill of choosing your thoughts. Let's turn our attention to this now, because being able to choose your thoughts and not get stuck in those ruminations or thought loops that can drag you down is so important to managing your anxiety and living a happy life.

You are a thinker.

**OBSERVE
THE THINKER
THINK**

Here is where change begins.

Chapter Six

MEDITATION: AN ART AND LEARNED SKILL

Wait—don't roll your eyes just yet. You might think meditation is bogus, or you may have tried it, not gotten results or felt like you failed and just dropped it. Bear with me and read through this section—then give it another try.

I want to start by mentioning that there are many types of meditation, and they all have slightly different goals and ways of practicing them. In ARP we need you to learn one key type (well, two, but let's start here!). You want to be able to become the Master of Choosing Your Thoughts. That is to say, you want to get really darn good at not letting those thought loops, ruminations or worries even get started, because once they do they can very quickly lead to panic attacks and high-level anxiety. But what if you saw a thought loop coming—like a train appearing miles down the track? Would that not be a lot easier to avoid than a train already barreling full speed into the station? What if the very first flash of that very first thought could be discarded, changed, or it could just float right on by you? If you could do this, you could avoid those anxiety-triggering thought loops.

Focal Point Meditation is a meditation I have specifically designed to accomplish just that: enable you to notice the very first inklings of a thought and then let the thought go, thus preventing that big nasty train from crashing into the station and wreaking havoc!

Meditation: the learned art of choosing your thoughts.

So many clients have told me they can't meditate because their minds race so fast, or they just naturally multitask. Others say they have Obsessive Compulsive Disorder so focusing is impossible. To all these folks I say, "Awesome! You are the most likely to learn quickly, and master, the art of choosing your thoughts!"

Why is this? Remember the three keys to neuroplastic change: Intention, Repetition and Reward. If you were to intentionally try to stay focused on one sensation—say, the feeling of your breath—and your thoughts kept going elsewhere, you would *repeatedly* have to choose to change your thoughts back to that sensation. And if your untrained mind wandered off hundreds of times, you'd have to choose hundreds of times more to bring it back to focus. Look at how many times you would be repeating the thought-change process. And since Repetition is one of the three keys to neuroplastic change, you would become like the athlete who never stops practicing to perfect her skills.

So if you are finding it challenging and uncomfortable to keep a singular focus (remember: Being uncomfortable is the harbinger of change!), then you are definitely on the right path.

I don't know a single successful and effective anxiety therapist who does not integrate some form of meditation into their treatment plans. It is common sense for any anxiety sufferer to learn how to manage their thoughts, since anxiety is rooted in how and what we think. So maybe it is time to figure out how to choose what we think about. Meditation helps us do that.

If you already know you don't (or won't) like meditation, I invite you here to give up being right about it. Instead, I'm asking you to be *curious* and consider exploring this skill. You may think this is part of the new-agey "woo-woo" stuff. For this reason, therapists of all sorts often call meditation by different names and use different language when describing it. A spiritual or Christian counsellor might call it prayer. I know of a psychologist who works on a military forces base with soldiers and officers. She offers what she calls "mind control" classes. So consider using a term or language that works for you, and let's get this skill under your belt as soon as possible.

Meditation is not difficult, nor is there a wrong way to do it. It is simply a skill that with Intention, Repetition and Reward you can master. Just like learning to ski, let's start on the baby slopes before we jump out of a helicopter onto the side of Mount Everest!

One of the goals of mindfulness—the ability to be aware of what your brain is getting itself up to at any given time—is called *metacognition, meta* meaning "referring to self" and *cognition* being the "thought process." Metacognition is *the ability to watch your thought process*. Imagine yourself as a fly on the wall of the room you are now in as you read this book. As that little fly, you observe yourself below, sitting in the room, and you see your words and thoughts. Imagine reflecting on these words and thoughts. Do you like them? Do they serve you well? Are they going to get you into trouble?

And what if as the fly you are able to tell yourself as the human sitting there that a certain thought that showed up, or the sentence you were about to say, was really not in your best interest to share with others? Armed with that metacognition in the moment, you would then be able to choose another thought, and perhaps not say those words out loud. You could avoid a lot of trouble and prevent a lot of anxiety!

We all do this kind of external reflection or observation naturally, usually just after the fact. How many times have you slapped your forehead the next day and said, "I can't believe I said that/did that!" This is called *retrospect*. Sometimes it comes to us after a good night's sleep, and sometimes only moments after the action in question. For me, a quick retrospect came when I said to my partner as we headed out the door for dinner, "Are you going to wear that?" Lesson learned! And the lesson is this: The more we close the timing gap between our retrospect and action, the less painful the potential outcome. My evening would have been much more enjoyable if my fly on the wall had poked me and said, "Hey buddy, the thought you are having about that outfit—drop it fast!" (I can be a slow learner sometimes, because I can get lazy with the Repetition part, but this one stuck pretty quickly!)

What if you had a way to close the timing gap on your retrospect? Wouldn't it be handy to have those retrospective thoughts in the present? You might call it forethought, but in this case, it would be forethought deeply infused with an understanding of the likely outcome. If you could notice your thoughts as they arise, then you'd stand a chance to make a *choice*. Meditation is how we learn to notice our thoughts in order to do this.

So let's get started.

Focal Point Meditation

For this exercise, it might be helpful to imagine a wide, invisible river filled with an infinite number of thoughts flowing above your head—a thought stream, so to speak. Like fish jumping randomly out of the river, thoughts drop out of the thought stream and into your head. Mindfulness gives you the ability to see a thought dropping in and make an instant decision to keep it or toss it back into the river. Since the thoughts are random, and you invest no time in them, they are neither good nor bad, just thoughts.

Can you invest six minutes a day in this practice? Wait, let's make this easier. How about two minutes, three times a day? And let's do two out of three of those times in bed so you really only need to figure out a two-minute slot once a day. Easy, right?

Here is all you have to do. Really it is not tricky; it is just a matter of Intention, Repetition and Reward (you saw that coming, didn't you!).

Since you are going to do this same practice three times a day, let's start with your morning.

The Two-Minute Meditation in Five Simple Steps

1. Set a timer for two minutes. You might want to download two minutes of white noise on your phone so you don't have to manage the thought, *Is the two minutes up yet?* I use the alarm on my smart phone, but even an egg timer will do.

2. Sit on the edge of your bed in an upright and dignified position. You can't manage your thoughts with Intention if you fall back asleep! Gently close your eyes to help block out visual distractions.

3. Take three very deep breaths, in through your nose and out through your mouth. Notice that the air going up your nostrils feels cooler than the air you exhale since it has not yet had a chance to be warmed by your body.*

4. Continue to breathe naturally and stay focused on the cool feeling of the breath entering your body. Every time a

thought about anything intrudes on your focus (your mind wanders), simply remove that thought by bringing your attention back to the cool feeling in your nose.

5. When the timer goes off, open your eyes, cross your arms across your chest, smile, and give yourself a good double pat on the back for doing your two-minute practice and just being you! (This is called the *Butterfly Hug.* It serves to help you experience Reward and Gratitude for these two minutes.)

   *Some people may not feel the temperature difference; not everyone's temperature sensors in their noses are sensitive. If this is the case for you, simply choose something else to focus on (something not uncomfortable). Perhaps you might put the palm of your hand on your thigh and notice the warmth between your palm and leg, or hold a stone or amulet in your hand to focus on that sensation.

Repeat this process at night before you lie down to go to sleep, and find two minutes midday to do the same. Find a place to be alone for your two minutes and use ear plugs or headphones to block out external noise that might prompt thoughts. A good place to be alone might be the comfort of a bathroom toilet stall. (People tend to leave you alone there to do your thing!)

Some days, you might find that your head is really busy. You might find that thoughts drop in and show up in a constant flow and that you need to pull your attention back to your breath dozens, if not hundreds, of times. Good for you; you're getting in lots of Repetition and practice. Other times you might find your head is a little less busy. It's all good. As long as you are intentionally bringing your thoughts back to your focal point and repeating that process, you are well on your way to mastering the art of choosing your thoughts. Don't forget the

Butterfly Hug at the end of every meditation. You need that little feeling of Reward to help lock in the rewiring.

There are so many solid clinical reasons this simple process can help end your panic attacks and manage your anxiety. Meditation is one essential tool you *cannot* do without. After all, it is those thoughts in that thought stream that run wild in your head and ramp up your anxiety. Therefore, learning how to drop a thought, change a thought, and decide whether or not to keep a thought just makes good sense.

A key to managing any superpower, is to be present with your thought in the moment.

On the next page, you can see the stages of mindfulness development. To end your panic attacks and live a life in which your anxiety levels are acceptable, helpful and manageable requires you to ultimately get to stage three, being *Mindful*, although you will quickly notice relief long before you master that stage.

The Stages of Mindfulness

MindLess

- Fully automatic thought process
- No perceived control over thoughts
- Experience is a victim of thoughts

MindFULL

- Beginning to notice your thoughts
- Occassionally choose to change or drop a thought
- Occassional moments of chosen experience

Mindful

- Regularly noticing your thoughts
- Regularly choosing to retain or discard thoughts and make a new positive thought
- Regular moments of chosen experience

Mindfullness

- Thoughts regularly appear that fit your practiced intention
- All thoughts are easily, readily and automatically changed if not suitable
- You are living a stress-free life of intention

A second type of meditation is also very helpful for anyone learning to manage anxiety. This very common type of meditation is simply about *calming down*. I get it, and I've said it before: No one in the history of calming down has ever calmed down by being told to calm down! This is not that.

This is a meditation that targets physical aspects of our body, like breathing. We know from scientific research that these physical functions are both a *product* of our good old amygdala and that they also *inform* our amygdala. Consequently, physical events are not just symptoms of anxiety, but can also be triggers for it. Oh, Homer, you and I are pretty wound up in each other!

Bringing your attention to physical sensations can help you calm your body. Do you remember the physical outcomes of Homer flooding you with adrenaline and cortisol? Two of the most significant of those outcomes have to do with the heart and the breath. So let's start with your breath and a breathing meditation.

Cardiac Coherence and Pranayama

Cardiac Coherence is a form of deep breathing that helps your heart and lungs work together to create a relaxed state of balance in your body. It has a direct impact on hormones that effect your stress and relaxation levels, including cortisol. Pranayama is a Sanskrit word that means *breath control* and is often used in yoga.

How to perform Cardiac Coherent breathing with Pranayama:

1. Start by taking six deep breaths per minute, one full inhale and exhale every 10 seconds:

    Inhale by filling your belly first, then your rib cage and chest.

    Exhale by pushing the air out of your chest and ribs,

and then your belly.

2. Repeat this inhale-exhale at least 20 times. You can use your fingers to help you count, or try any popular app that helps you time your breathing. Breathe as deeply as you can and keep a rhythmic flow going.

3. For increased effectiveness, incorporate a form of yogic breathing called *Pranayama*. Alternate nostrils on the inhale and exhale by pinching closed one nostril and then the other:

   Inhale left, hold for four, exhale right. Inhale right, hold for four, exhale left. Repeat.

Just 3-5 minutes of this deep breathing stimulates sense receptors in your heart's aorta that send messages to your brain and endocrine system. Endorphins and *acetylcholine* (a neurotransmitter) are released into your bloodstream with positive effects that include an ensuing sense of calm lasting about four hours. Stress hormones such as cortisol are decreased.

Some benefits of Cardiac Coherence:

- Reduces stress and lowers blood pressure
- Calms and relaxes
- Relieves pain
- Alleviates depression
- Reduces addictive behaviour
- Improves memory and mental alertness
- Increases energy levels

An increased oxygen level will both relax *and* energize you. Oxygen is a key to life, it feeds every cell in your body and your cells and organs use it to regenerate and revitalize, and when well-saturated with oxygen they expend less energy to function. I recommend this practice three times per day: when you get up, midday and in the evening. If you are doing your Focal Point Meditation at these times, you may incorporate this as a warm-up to the mediation. Also, use it spontaneously during the day whenever you feel the need to settle some inbound anxiety or just want to centre yourself

Reaching a life of *Mindfulness* is pretty awesome, and it can take years of Intention, Repetition and Reward to get there. Buddhist monks and old sages commit their life to this art. But don't worry, a panic attack-free life with an appropriate level of helpful anxiety does not require anywhere near that level of mastery.

Meditation is very popular these days, and now you know why. It is an important part of ARP. Since it requires little skill, no equipment and can be done anywhere, it is neither expensive nor difficult to practice.

In your community there are likely resources to help you connect with others interested in mediation and learn more about, and practice, this skill. If you want to go to the masters, contact your local Buddhist temple—most offer free programs to teach meditation (usually with no uncomfortable pressure to become involved in the faith). Schools, community centres, universities and medical clinics all frequently offer courses on, or gatherings for, meditation.

The more practice you get in, the quicker you will master this skill. Team up with a friend, family member or partner who also wants to manage their stress and anxiety, and get them doing their three, two-minute meditations a day—and keep each other motivated.

You'll both be grateful. And I have a lot more to say about the benefits of gratitude.

BE GRATEFULNESS

It slays monsters and tames dragons.

Chapter Seven

GRATITUDE THERAPY

If I had to pick just one therapy modality that has had the biggest, most sustained impact in my life and in the lives of my clients, it would absolutely be *Gratitude Therapy*. I have used this form of therapy for individuals, couples, people with PTSD, anxiety and depression, and heck, I think just about *every one* of my clients has had some form Gratitude Therapy in their personal care program.

Since you have been reading carefully, you have likely already figured out why. Gratitude is a key component to neuroplastic change, and I have been referring to it as Reward. If you want change, you need to always pay attention to those three underlying components. (Do I have to repeat this one again?!) The purpose of Gratitude Therapy is to rewire your brain to become a master at noticing the good stuff. We all have that one friend who can drive us a bit crazy with their constant positivity. Maybe they have a bubbly personality and at times can even seem detached from reality. I had a childhood friend Julia who was like this. She could show up hungry at a gourmet buffet where there was nothing left but a picked-over veggie tray, and she'd exclaim, "Perfect! I love vegetarianism. And this is *sooooo* good for me!" Yeah, I know. But there is a lot to be admired about a brain that, even in the face of a drought, sees the cup as half full.

The *Negative Evolutionary Bias* we spoke about early in this book programs us to be exactly the opposite of grateful. In a drought (and as a general default), we naturally see the glass as half empty. Our survival may be contingent upon our ability to prevent the glass from becoming empty, so our bias ensures we set our minds in advance to the problem of how we'd survive this worst-case scenario.

Gratitude Therapy is designed to rewire those neurons to notice the things in life that bring you feelings of joy and pleasure. Anxiety doesn't stand much chance of gaining momentum in your brain when you are feeling joy!

The endgame here is to build neuronal connections that notice Gratitude, the same way you would build the muscles in your throwing arm if you wanted to be a professional baseball pitcher. The more time you spend actively noticing things that make you grateful, the less time you spend trashing the present moment with those *Fictional Events Appearing Real*.

There is an entire book to be written on Gratitude Therapy, and many therapists have made entire careers out of various forms of it. I offer it to you as a necessary part of the ARP.

It begins with a simple little exercise that I would invite you to share with your partner, family or bestie. It's simple to do, takes little time and can help you make profound gains in your effort to lower your anxiety.

Grab yourself a lined notebook from a dollar store or a fancy one from the bookstore. It doesn't matter, but if you keep this exercise up over time—as you should!—it's nice to compile a series of these books for your library.

Each and every morning, before you leave your bedroom, make a list of at least five things for which you are grateful.

(As you can see, we are building a morning routine here, meditation, pranayama, meditation and gratitude lists—and routine tends to minimize anxiety.)

The items on your list don't have to be big, they don't have to be related, and they don't have to be things you possess. They can be people, things, feelings, behaviours, responses, presumptions—it can be just about *anything.* They just need to be things you are even a little bit grateful to encounter in your life.

The items *must* be different every day. Never repeat something already on the list, as the objective of this exercise is to encourage your subconscious to build neuropathways that are consistently looking for points of Gratitude. The brain is an efficiency machine, and if your morning requires a ton of brainpower (energy) to come up with this list, the brain will find an easier way—gathering the items for your list during your day. In effect, we start to become that person that notices Gratitude often, and when we are grateful it is darned difficult to be anxious!

List those five different things in your book, and if you are inspired, write a sentence or two of reflection about one of them.

Here's one of my recent entries:

I'm grateful for:

1. The ton of writing I did yesterday
2. My new web host
3. Warmer weather
4. Fresh sheets
5. Waking early
6. Squirrels

A Brief Reflection: I decided to try to finish the book yesterday and I came very darn close! I wrote a lot. It feels great to have the end in sight and know I am soon going to be able to share this information with thousands of people.

Sometimes I put down more than five things. When I find five come easily, I continue to list more until my brain has to work a little harder, forcing those neurons to search and stretch a bit. It is much like doing those additional reps at the gym when lifting weights: It is the extra push that makes the biggest difference.

At the end of your day, just before you turn off the lights and put your head on the pillow, read *out loud* what you wrote that morning. If you have a partner to read it to, awesome, and if not, it is fine to read it out loud to your dog, cat or the universe! *Just read it out loud*.

Over time, and possibly in short order, you will begin to notice your Gratitude muscle (those growing neuronal connections in your brain that notice things for which you are thankful) alerting you to these points of Gratitude quite unexpectedly, and seemingly quite randomly. For example, you might find yourself on your usual walk to lunch when suddenly your brain shouts at you: "Squirrel! They are cute little things, and they are going on tomorrow's list!"

In a very cool way, you might actually get Homer to work *for* you, should you find some *positive* anxiety attached to keeping the daily commitment to write your list. This is Homer, ever looking out for you, giving you enough of a poke to change your thoughts and notice something that will prepare you for success in the future. Now look at that: We are not only no longer fighting with Homer, we can actually be grateful for him (you could even add him to your list!).

Over time, this wonderful little exercise builds neuronal pathways so strong that they hum along all day.

One of my clients loved the outcome of this exercise so much he turned it into a family ritual. He had a beautiful antique wooden lectern he'd bought from a church that was closing. He installed the lectern at his front door and instituted a new family rule: As each member of the family came home at the end of their day, they were to enter into the *Family Gratitude Journal* at least one thing they were grateful for that day. At first his teenaged twin daughters weren't so excited about Dad adding homework, but over time the entire family embraced the family journal project with pride.

Working with hundreds of clients over the years, I have created a daily five-step plan that I encouraged all of them—and now *you*—to embrace. The Gratitude Therapy exercise I just shared with you comprises *step one* and *five* of the plan:

1. Write your gratitude list in the morning.
2.
3.
4.
5. In the evening, read your gratitude list out loud.

As you may be beginning to see, everything we are doing in this book is not just about ending your panic attacks and managing your anxiety. It is about *intentionally creating the life you both want and deserve*. It is about making choices to become someone you are proud of and happy to be.

Steps two to four of this daily plan incorporate practices you learned above. All of the steps tap into changing important parts of your life by having you Intentionally, and with Repetition and Gratitude, *become* those things the steps encourage.

Here is "The Daily 5" in its entirety. Copy it, post it on your fridge and get the whole family involved. Trust me—this can be life changing!

The Daily Five *to Creating Happiness, Ending Depression and Making Lasting Positive Change*
Intention, Repetition & Reward/Gratitude

(These are the 3 components necessary to build new neuronal pathways.)

1. First thing in the morning, *intentionally* journal 5+ *new* (different each day) things you are grateful for in your life (personal or business). If you choose, journal or write 1-3 short sentences about one of the items you listed. If you like to journal, go for a bit more.

   Give yourself a pat on the back each and every time you do this step (this is the *Gratitude* part!).

2. *Intentionally* meditate: Do a short, two-minute meditation three times per day. Set a timer or download two minutes of white noise on your phone or iPod, sit in a quiet place and simply focus on one sensation. I suggest focusing on the temperature change that occurs in your nostrils as you breathe in and out.

   As your attention drifts or other thoughts drop into your head, just acknowledge them and return your attention to the temperature change (or whatever you're focusing on). Some days this will happen a lot, and some days very little. Both experiences are good.

   Give yourself a pat on the back each and every time you do this step (this is the *Gratitude* part!).

3. *Intentionally* do something good for your body. Yes I know, exercise might be something you have tried and found difficult. If you don't hit the gym, schedule 20 minutes every day to "plank" and do jumping jacks, or to do some

other short exercise that both targets your core strength and gets your heart rate up. Or, make an *intentional* choice to have a salad instead of the burger, or take the stairs instead of the elevator.

Give yourself a pat on the back each and every time you do this step (this is the *Gratitude* part!).

4. Perform an *intentional* act of kindness every day. I suggest writing one brief email per day to someone in your life (again personal or professional) thanking them for who they are, what they have done or how they make a difference to you. As an alternative, make it a point to buy a homeless person a coffee or even lunch.

   Give yourself a pat on the back each and every time you do this step (this is the *Gratitude* part!).

5. Just before bed, *intentionally* read to yourself out loud, or someone else, the gratitude list you wrote in *step one*.

Give yourself a pat on the back each and every day you complete these five steps.

If you commit to, and *do,* these five simple things daily, I can assure you that you will experience a positive change in your life. Couple this tool with insightful coaching/therapy and you will find that you are able to manage anxiety, overcome depression and begin to live a much more fulfilling and happy life.

Life is suffering.

CHOOSE

if you want to suffer in response.

Chapter Eight

COGNITIVE BEHAVIOURAL THERAPY WITH ARP

Cognitive Behavioral Therapy is a therapy technique that has been around for a few decades now, is well tested, and has plenty of research to back its effectiveness in many circumstances. CBT helps you challenge the negative thoughts about yourself and others that lead you (and likely others) to unnecessary anxiety. By examining your thinking and considering alternative thoughts, you can come to happier and healthier conclusions. If you do this often enough with Intention, Repetition and Reward, you become someone who can easily see and embrace the thoughts that help you end panic attacks and manage your anxiety.

CBT is the go-to strategy for many therapists, as it is easily learned and is taught to therapists in most every comprehensive therapy training program. Clients respond well if they do their homework.

In ARP we integrate a simple form of CBT in an easy-to-use format that reflects what you now know about neuroplasticity, and how to manage your anxiety in a compassionate and effective way.

CBT does require some journaling or charting, so if that's not your thing you might find this modality tedious. The benefit of putting our thoughts on paper, however, is that it helps us look at *how* we think and view making changes to our thinking as a manageable project. So, CBT is very much worth trying, at least for a couple of weeks. In addition to the benefits of the CBT itself, this process will give you a record of how you were feeling that you can reflect upon at a later date for the specific purpose of ingraining that sense of Reward as ARP takes effect. Reward is so important in locking in your neuroplastic change.

Create your own CBT Record sheet. Simply divide a page into 7 columns labelled:

1. When, Where (Situation)
2. Homer's Thoughts
3. Anxiety Rating 1-10
4. Safety Thoughts after Key Phrases
   (Homer, you want my attention, you've got it.
   Homer, you want to keep me safe, I am going to help.)
5. Realistic Outcomes and Conclusions
6. Anxiety Rating 1-10

You can fill this sheet out either when your anxiety is elevated or after the anxiety is gone. If you feel you are moving towards a panic attack, focus on working with Homer first, and ensure he is feeling heard and safe and that your cortisol levels have stabilized or dropped before doing paperwork!

After you fill out your chart, review your *before* and *after* numbers from columns 3 and 6. Do the Butterfly Hug and spend a minute or two with any positive outcome to help embed the Reward component associated with your improved change.

On the following pages is an example of an ARP/CBT Journal.

CBT and the ARP

CBT is the technique used most often by psychologists, as it is the modality most often taught if they choose to train in psychotherapy. Because CBT is based on parsing your thoughts in a sequential and logical way, people who have logical brains respond well. If you are not one of these people, you probably know one! Opposites attract, and often in relationships we find one person who is very logical (sometimes introverted) and a partner who seems to be relatively much less organized or creative (and sometimes extroverted). Neither is better than the other—it is just how we are wired.

Personally, I am not wired for linear thinking. Spreadsheets, multiple choice exams, and logic puzzles are my personal hell. My brain loves to operate out of the box and be spontaneous. Consequently, although I appreciate and value CBT, it is not a large part of what made the ARP successful in managing my own anxiety.

You, however, may love this stuff! Dig into this CBT and see how it feels. It may fit like a glove, or not. And both outcomes are OK. Hopefully, if you took to heart my challenge earlier to give up being right in favour of being curious, you have indulged the strategies in each chapter with an open curiosity. At this point, you have the necessary skills to invest deeply in the parts of the ARP that that make sense to your brain. CBT might be one of them.

WHEN/WHERE SITUATION	HOMER'S THOUGHTS	ANXIETY RATING (1-10)

SAFETY THOUGHTS (AFTER KEY PHRASES)	REALISTIC OUTCOMES AND CONCLUSIONS	ANXIETY RATING (1-10)

CULTIVATE INSIGHT

Exchange being right
for being curious.

Chapter Nine

TAPPING
PART ONE

How to Physically Lower Your Stress Hormones

Sweaty palms, racing heart, tight throat, an awful feeling in your gut, the urge to run: You now know these are the effects of high levels of adrenaline and cortisol in your system (and by now I hope you have stopped calling them the symptoms of anxiety!). It does not matter if Homer, the guy or gal in your amygdala, threw open the tap and flooded you, or if someone injected you with these hormones through an IV or syringe, the hormones are creating the sensations of anxiety, and it's the hormones we need to deal with.

If you were to feel these effects because someone opened the flow on your IV, close it and the symptoms disappear. Similarly, if you're feeling the symptoms because of Homer, you need to convince him to shut off the cortisol. We have already talked about how to work with Homer to stop him from working so hard: Give him what he wants.

"Homer, you wanted my attention, you got it!

"Homer, you want to keep me safe, I am going to help."

There is a second way of getting Homer to cooperate and back off with the flow of adrenaline and cortisol, and it is very practical technique, whether you are in a corporate boardroom, a packed elevator or anyplace where talking to your amygdala out loud might feel a bit awkward. And since we can measure hormone levels in the body, researchers have been able to test the following technique and have learned that it does indeed drop adrenaline and cortisol levels.

Remember Sarah and Dan, our soon-to-be newlyweds in Chapter One? Sarah had a major panic attack just as she was about to walk up the aisle to marry the love of her life. I've seen many panic attacks in my personal and professional life, and Sarah's was up there in the top three. Dear, sweet Sarah was on the floor, sobbing and trying to catch her breath, and was so convinced she was dying that she begged for an ambulance. And yet, less than ten minutes later, she was composed enough to recite her vows to Dan in front of 500 people.

I am the kind of guy who believes in miracles—it comes as part of my jobs—but this was no miracle. Sarah's recovery happened because I coached her right then and there in a technique called *Tapping*, or *Emotional Freedom Technique* (EFT—not to be confused with *Emotionally Focused Therapy*, which is not part of the ARP).

Tapping is based in both Eastern and Western medicine. In Eastern medicine, the use of acupuncture (and acupressure) has been around for centuries. Records of its use and application have been traced back to about 350 B.C.E., and there is archeological evidence that it may have been used as early as the Stone Age. Anything that's been around that long and is still being taught in medical schools must have something going for it! And from a Western medical perspective, we can measure hormone levels in the body and, as I noted earlier, we can consistently see the two stress hormones dropping when we apply this technique.

So, whether we look at this technique from an Eastern or a Western perspective, it is proven to *work*.

Just ask Sarah and Dan.

The moment I entered Sarah's dressing room and saw her on the floor sobbing and surrounded by the ladies in her wedding party, I was quite certain what was happening. Her mom's quick reply to my inquiry had confirmed Sarah was in a full-on panic attack.

Convincing all of those ladies to leave Sarah alone with me was right up there with getting between a momma bear and her cub! But with a warm and reassuring voice I kept repeating to her protectors, "I really know how to help Sarah. I promise I can make her feel OK." One by one the ladies left and I got to work.

I quickly checked in with Sarah to make sure she did indeed want to marry Dan that day. I wanted to rule out the possibility that she had a valid reason to be frightened to walk down that aisle. (I had never officiated a shotgun wedding, and Sarah's was not about to be my first!)

With Sarah's confirmation that she did indeed want to get married, I immediately launched into Tapping. This was an emergency that required immediate corrective action, and Tapping is a protocol in which I'd had a great deal of experience and which I knew could make a difference very quickly.

I'll finish telling you the details of Sarah's story and then walk you through the very simple steps of Tapping so you can do it for yourself.

Recall this pivotal moment: "OK ,then, Sarah, I want you to pay really close attention to me. I want you to repeat everything I say and everything I do. Can you do that?"

Sarah nodded, yet continued to hyperventilate between sobbing and tears.

I began tapping three fingers on the outside edge of my

hand, below the pinky, or as I call it in order to lighten the moment, the *Karate Chop* point. Sarah did not immediately copy me, so I took her hands and helped her copy my action. "Keep tapping there," I said, "and repeat after me."

The Set-up Phrase (one of the first steps) was critical. It needed to be powerful, yet not too scary, and very short and direct. I also wanted it to incorporate humorous exaggeration because laughter, if I could provoke it, is such a powerful way to drop cortisol levels. I said to her, "If I walk up that aisle today, I'm going to pass out cold and wake up dead!"

Sarah looked at me a bit puzzled, her brain trying to devote resources to figuring out whether the guy who was supposed to officiate her wedding was crazy, which in turn redirected her brain's resources away from her all-consuming thoughts of anxiety.

Here's why a little offbeat humour works so well in dropping cortisol levels during a panic attack: Our brains don't multi-task. Multi-tasking is a myth bosses use to make people feel guilty about not getting enough done! In reality, our brains switch from one thought to another and back again at such lightning speed that we only *think* we are retaining multiple thoughts concurrently. However, we're not wired to be able to hold more than one conscious thought at a time.

"Keep tapping, Sarah." With all that was going on in her head at that moment, I needed to coach her brain to stay on track. "And repeat what I just said: If I walk up that aisle today, I am going to pass out cold and wake up dead."

Sarah did as she was directed and pushed out a teary, sobbing version of the Set-up Phrase.

Then I said, "And, I completely and totally love and respect myself. Say it, Sarah. Repeat everything I say!"

And she did.

"OK, repeat it again and keep tapping!" I continued to show Sarah where to tap, a series of other places on her body (I'll tell you what they are in the next chapter) that I knew lowered cortisol levels. I also continued coaching her to repeat: "If I walk up that aisle today, I'm going to pass out cold and wake up dead, and I completely and totally love and respect myself."

As she repeated the statement and continued tapping, a small smile cracked through Sarah's sobs as it sunk in that what I had her saying sounded so very ridiculous!

We didn't stop yet. It's difficult to tap and talk and hyperventilate all at once, and her brain was being forced to devote resources to the Tapping process, which stimulated the lowering of her adrenaline and cortisol. She stopped sobbing and started breathing more normally.

"That's crazy," she interjected, "I'm not going to wake up dead!"

I chuckled and refocused her on the Tapping exercise. I needed to get her hormone levels low enough that she would not revert to panic if she stopped. I took her through the cycle of Tapping locations three more times. She started showing signs of composure. then had her complete the last few steps in the protocol, connecting the sensation of calm with the thought of walking down the aisle.

Sarah took the last few deep breaths to complete the process. "You know, Sarah, I think all that energy you just shifted is really just the huge bundle of love you have to give your new husband—let's call it your superpower!" I gave her the biggest, most loving smile I could and said, "So, you ready to marry that man?!"

She tried to give me a big hug and I stopped her. "Save that for your hubby! Shall we walk up that aisle?"

Sarah laughed and took my hand, and I walked her across the huge reception hall to the door of the wedding room. She waited, all smiles, at the end of the aisle as I proceeded towards a very relieved-looking Dan. I turned to face their friends and family, the music shifted and I loudly proclaimed, "Ladies and gentlemen, please stand for the entrance of the bride!"

I love my jobs. ☺

Worries are thought loops
stuck in your head.

BREAKING THE LOOP

is a learned skill.

Chapter Ten

TAPPING
PART TWO

The Technique

OK. Now that you know why this technique works, let's get down to the details of how it's done, and it is not complicated. Like any neuroplastic change in our brain, it simply takes Intention, Repetition and Reward.

Tapping is most easily used when your anxiety is in response to clear and identifiable triggers such as the thought of getting on an airplane, the sight of a snake or the anticipation of having to speak in public. It can, however, also be successfully used for more complex situations, and for these I would suggest working with a therapist who is an experienced Tapping practitioner. As I mentioned earlier, Tapping is also called *Emotional Freedom Technique* or *EFT* (again, not to be confused with EFT: Emotional Focused Therapy, a different modality).

Let's walk through the 8 steps of the ARP Tapping

technique, using a fear of snakes as our example. When you tap on the various body locations in the protocol, it does not matter which side of the body you tap on. Use three fingers (you stand a better chance of hitting the specific point) and tap firmly enough to feel it but not so hard that it hurts. (We are not trying to beat the anxiety out of you here; Homer would not take kindly to that approach!)

Step 1: Entry Grading

As you now know, Reward/Gratitude is one of the three elements of creating neuroplastic change. You'll need a clear, measurable indicator of how well the Tapping process is working, so you can invest Reward in your improvement.

Find a quiet place and sit in a comfortable and upright position. Privacy is best; it is ideal to speak aloud the phrases as you master this process.

Reflect on the last time you were freaked out about being in the presence of a snake (or a loud, angry dog or any other animal that scared you). Really go there: Relive that moment, recalling as many details as you can, where you were, the time of day, who was with you, the sight, colour, shape of the beast and any sounds or smells. Really invest in the memory, and yes, this will ramp up your anxiety, and that is OK.

Once you really feel as if you are re-experiencing the moment, grade your fear on a scale. Ask yourself: "As I reflect now, in this moment, on the thought of being exposed to this snake, how upsetting is it on a scale from 0-10, zero being I could not care less, and ten being flat-out panic?"

Note this number. It should ideally be above 6. If it is lower than this, you can still continue to work on the issue, but note that the drop in anxiety may not feel as dramatic.

Step 2: The Set-up Phrase

Begin by tapping on the *Karate Chop* point, the outside of either hand. While continuously tapping on the *Karate Chop* point, repeat this phrase 3 times:

> *"Even though I am terrified of seeing a snake*, I deeply and completely love and accept myself."*
>
> *Insert your chosen issue.

If you are *not* dealing with extreme anxiety (8+ grade) you can modify the Set-up Phrase as you tap by exaggerating it, even to comical extremes such as I did with Sarah by stating she would "wake up dead!" For example, "Every time I think about a snake, I get such crazy anxiety my heart actually jumps right out of my chest!"

Express aloud the exaggerated anxiety of the event, ending the sentence with: "And I deeply and completely love and accept myself."

Repeat this Set-up Phrase three times while continuously tapping through the following sequence of points on the body.

Step 3: The Sequence

While tapping about five times on each of these 14 points, repeat the Set-up Phrase three times while tapping on each point.

These are the points (you will find them illustrated at the end of this chapter):

1. Very top of your head
2. Inner end of your eyebrow
3. Just to the outside of your eye
4. Under your eye close to your tear duct

5. Under your nose above your upper lip
6. Under your lower lip halfway down your chin
7. Top of your sternum, just below your collar bone in the centre of your chest
8. The "bra strap" point—reach around your torso and tap where your bra strap might be if you wore one (sorry, gentlemen!)
9. The wrist, on the inside of your arm about three finger widths up from the crease where your hand meets your wrist
10. Karate Chop point—the fleshy side of your hand
11. Inside of your baby finger on the fleshy part beside your fingernail
12. Inside of your middle finger (skip your ring finger) on the fleshy part beside your fingernail
13. Inside of your index finger on the fleshy part beside your fingernail
14. Inside of your thumb on the fleshy part beside your fingernail.

Step 4: The 10 Gamut

Perform these next 10 actions (below), while continuously tapping the Gamut Point (a point on the back of your hand—see the EFT InfoGraphic.):

1. Close your eyes.
2. Open your eyes.
3. Hold your head steady and look hard down to right.
4. Hold your head steady and look hard down to left.
5. Roll your eyes in a complete circle clockwise.
6. Roll your eyes in a complete circle counterclockwise.
7. Sing the first verse of "Happy Birthday."
8. Count from 5 down to 1.
9. Sing the first verse of "Happy Birthday" again.

10. Place your hands on the top of your thighs and take 3 very slow deep breaths through your nose.

Step 5: Exit Grading

Reflect again on the same incident you began with and ask yourself the identical question:

> "As I reflect now, in this moment, on the thought of being exposed to this snake, how upsetting is it on a scale from 0-10, zero being I could not care less, and ten being flat out panic?"

Again, grade the anxiety from 1-10, and note any improvement. If it has dropped even one number, that is a 10 percent difference! Take a moment to appreciate the change.

> If the anxiety is still above 3, move on to Step 6.
> If the anxiety is below 3, move directly to Step 8.

Step 6: Revise Step 3: The Sequence

Repeat *Step 3* but change your language to preface your statements with "Even though I *still* experience a bit of anxiety when I see a snake, I deeply and completely love and accept myself."

Step 7: Grade the Anxiety 1-10

Grade the anxiety again. If the anxiety is now below 3, take a moment to congratulate yourself! Then move on to *Step 8*.

If the anxiety is still above 3, move back to *Step 6*, and repeat until the anxiety drops below 3.

Step 8: Celebrate (Reward in Neuroplastic Change)

The brain will work hard to repeat good feelings, so take a few moments to savour your results.

Notice that a drop of 3 points is almost *one third*, and *5 points* means you dropped your anxiety *in half!* That is *impressive!* No drugs; no therapist; just you and an easy, repeatable technique called Tapping. Well done! You managed this success all on your own. Notice that, and be happy and grateful for this amazing outcome. Maximize that feeling of Reward.

While doing the Butterfly Hug, say out loud an affirmation that acknowledges what you've accomplished. For example: "My anxiety is quite manageable while I'm in the presence of a snake."

Recall that the Butterfly Hug is a simple position where you cross your arms across your chest and reach around to your back as far as you can comfortably go. Pat your back with your hands, alternating sides with each pat.

Like any new skill done with Intention, Repetition and Reward, your body and mind will quickly learn the dependable outcome of this process: a drop in cortisol and the ensuing feeling of calm and presence, even in the face of old anxiety triggers. You may find that once you have used this technique many times over, your body responds more and more quickly, and sometimes the initial Karate Chop point is sufficient to drop your cortisol to an acceptable level.

How often should you practice this technique?

Often. You know Repetition is essential to mastering any skill and integrating it into your life. When you start Tapping, I suggest you practice this technique dozens of times a day. I know that sounds like a lot, but it is simple *cause and effect*: The more you practice (Repetition), the more experience your mind and body will have lowering your cortisol levels. After all, if your anxiety is enough of an issue you are investing time to read this book and or go to therapy, this proven technique is well worth the time investment. And, after all, this is your endgame: to become really good at lowering your levels of stress hormones and keeping them at manageable levels.

Now that you understand a bit about how the brain works and how to change its wiring, you can understand how and why this Tapping technique works. If you apply the three necessary elements of neuroplastic change, you will find that the body and brain will give you even better results, and do so more quickly. It is not uncommon, and can even be expected, that if you apply these techniques with Intention, Repetition and Reward long enough and frequently enough, your body will begin to respond when you simply hold the Intention. In other words, with enough practice, just thinking about reducing your cortisol levels can reduce your anxiety.

There is many a Toronto executive who, in a meeting, appears to have a simple nervous tick of tapping on a particular point of their body (often the Karate Chop point). You may even see folks riding the subway doing the same thing. Many of these people are former clients of mine who learned this technique through individual sessions or at one of my workshops, or from one of the hundreds of therapists I have trained.

Tapping can be so powerfully life changing I encourage you to really invest in this technique. There are multiple websites and experienced Tapping Practitioners you can find on line, including on YouTube. This is a safe, fun modality and I encourage you to continue to do research and practice often.

Although I kicked my own panic attacks decades ago, I still use this technique regularly. Whenever I notice my anxiety rising—even just a little bit—I tap. If I know I am about to experience a situation or be in close proximity to a person that can or used to ramp me up, I tap. It's as good a preventative measure as it is as a cure!

an integration between Western medicine (Exposure Therapy) & Eastern medicine (Acupressure).

Emotional Freedom Technique or 'Tapping'

Step 1 ENTRY GRADING

Recall or create that feeling of anxiety around the issue and grade it (1 - 10).

Step 2 THE SET-UP PHRASE

While continuously Tapping on the Karate Chop Point (KC), Repeat this phrase 3 times:

"Even though I have/am ______________,
I deeply & completely love and accept myself."

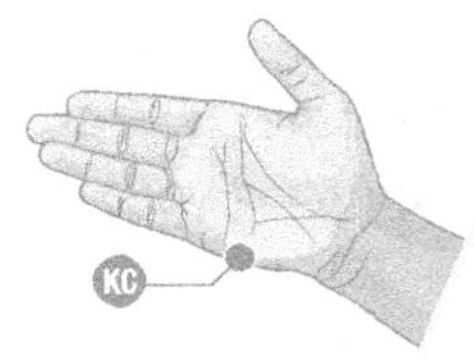

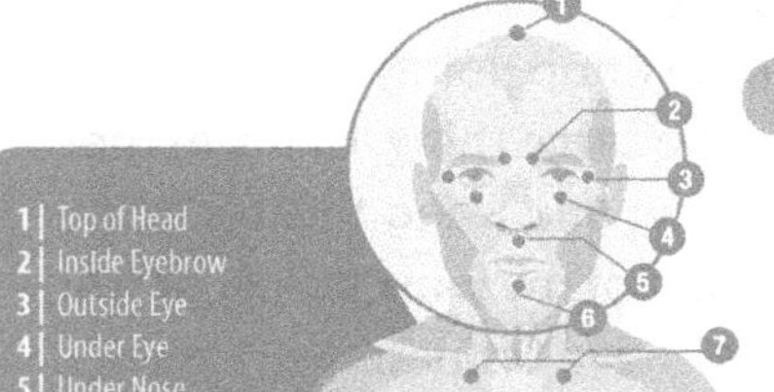

Step 3 THE SEQUENCE

While tapping about (**5x**) on each of the (**14 points**), Express aloud the exaggerated* anxiety of the event, ending each sentence with...

"and I deeply and completely love & accept myself."

(e.g. Every time I think about flying, I get such crazy anxiety, my heart actually jumps right out of my chest!")

*If the anxiety when you are about to tap is extreme, tone down the Initial Statement, simply repeating the **SET-UP PHRASE** through each point.

Step 4 THE 10 GAMUT

Perform these 10 actions while continuously tapping the Gamut Point.

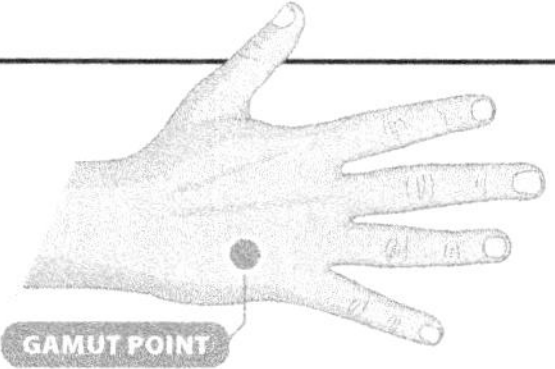

1. Eyes closed.
2. Eyes open.
3. Head steady, eyes hard down to RIGHT.
4. Head steady, eyes hard down to LEFT.
5. Roll eyes in complete circle.
6. Roll eyes in a complete circle in the opposite direction.
7. Sing the 1st verse of Happy Birthday.
8. Count from 5 back to 1.
9. Sing the 1st verse of Happy Birthday, again.
10. Place your hands on the top of your thighs & take 3 very slow deep breaths.

Step 5 EXIT GRADING

Grade the Anxiety (1-10)

If the anxiety is below 3, then take a moment to ***congratulate yourself!***

If the anxiety is still above three, move onto **STEP 6.**

Step 6

Repeat STEP 3, **'THE SEQUENCE'** & change your language to preface your statements with...

"Even though I STILL am experiencing a bit of this ______________, I deeply & completely love and accept myself."

Step 7

Grade the Anxiety (1-10)

If the anxiety is below 3, then take a moment to ***congratulate yourself!***

If the anxiety is still above three, move back to **STEP 6,** *and repeat until the anxiety dropes below 3.*

Step 8 CELEBRATE

The brain will work hard to repeat good feelings, so take a few moments to savour your results. Repeat an affirmation while doing the butterfly tap.

(With your arms tightly crossed over your chest, alternatively tap on your back with your full hand.)

"I am comfortable flying in a plane"

Dopamine is your brain's happy juice.

LAUGHTER RELEASES DOPAMINE

Guess what...

Chapter Eleven

THE EMOTIONS **WHEEL**

Becoming a Master of Changing Your Emotions

"Oh, I wish I didn't feel like this!" How many times have you said this to yourself? How many times have you tried to fight your way out of a funk? How many times have you wished you did not feel sad, mad, angry, jealous or a whole host of other emotions that, frankly, just feel like *crap?*

Too many times, if you are like most of us.

Emotions have two sources, and neither is outside of you. Nope, It's not your partner's doing, your teacher's doing, your parent's doing, nor anyone else's. Yes, others can seem like they cause the circumstances that lead to your emotional reaction, but the feelings you experience and the actions you respond with are all yours!

No one has enough power or magic to put a feeling or emotion into your head!

Emotions are a combination of resident thoughts in your own brain and the chemicals and hormones that create and support them. And that is *all in your head*. This is good news, because it means that with the right technique, just as you can change your cortisol levels and lower your anxiety, you can also change how you feel.

You might be thinking: "This sounds good, but if my partner sticks me with taking out a jam-packed trash can one more time...." This is *just* a thought, and if it were followed up by, or precipitated by, a feeling or emotion, you do have the power to shift both or either.

There is another piece of good news about our feelings and emotions: No individual feeling or emotion is ever permanent. *Impermanence* is a characteristic of all things, including what's going on in our heads. It is helpful to always remind ourselves that our miserable feelings won't last forever. When you are feeling good, savour it. When you are feeling less than good, remember Impermanence.

No emotion or feeling is ever permanent. Savour Impermanence, it helps us enjoy the good, and carries through the less than good.

This exercise I'll teach in this chapter is a powerful one you should consider mastering, as it can turn you into the *Master of Changing Your Emotions!*

Why are you reading suddenly about feelings, instead of panic attacks and anxiety? Depending on who you ask, thoughts create feelings or feelings create thoughts. Either way, what you think and how you feel are both pivotal to Homer's decisions about your cortisol levels. Consequently being able to manage your feelings can be as important as changing your thoughts when it comes to managing your anxiety.

Many of our emotions are very similar to each other, but if we take a moment to really pay attention to them, they do feel different. For example, think about the feeling of joy, then the feeling of happiness and finally the feeling of ecstasy. They all feel pretty good, but also a bit different. We have different words for them because they are more than just degrees of the same feeling.

When we apply Intention to changing how we feel, the easiest change comes when shifting our emotions from their current state to another emotion that feels pretty close to it, like changing from happiness to joy instead of from happiness to jealousy.

Imagine if you were an actor and the scene required you to be very angry at another character. You snarl your lines accordingly, and the director screams, "CUT! I don't want you just angrier, show me RAGE!" And since you are quite capable of giving Meryl Streep a run for her money, you launch back into the scene, and with terrifying believability, you RAGE!

Think about this change for a moment. Of course, there are days when an actor might not wake up feeling happy, angry or whatever emotion is required by the director and the script. But it is their job to step into that emotion, and if they can't or don't really become that emotion, we call it bad acting. Great actors deeply feel and experience, by choice, the emotion required for a scene. They have learned how to release just the right cocktail of chemicals and electrical impulses in their brain to experience it. Actors are not the only ones who can shift their feelings; we all can. It just takes, you guessed it: Intention, Repetition and Reward.

The Emotions Wheel

At the end of this passage you will find a list of feelings and emotions on a wheel, each similar to, but not the same as, the feeling next to it. In the centre of the wheel is a beautiful Sanskrit symbol that means Impermanence. People often look at this wheel and view it as a list of bad emotions and good emotions. For the purpose of this exercise, do your best to let go of that way of thinking, and try, as best you can, not to place judgment or value on any of the emotions. There is no doubt that feeling happy beats feeling sad (and sometimes sadness is appropriate); but, in this exercise, it is important not to judge any emotion on the list. What matters is learning to shift from one emotion to the next as you move around the circle—until you've become a Master of Changing Your Emotions!

Some of the shifts will be a bit easier than others. You can step on the wheel at whatever emotion you are feeling in that moment. If you are feeling frustrated, start there, or happy, or wherever. Now *choose* to move in either direction on the wheel. (Yes, it is easy to judge the next emotion or feeling and want to move to the more enjoyable one, but sometimes we find that more difficult than moving in the other direction—either is fine.) Remember, the goal here is to become *Master* of Changing Your Emotions. It is the *change* we are trying to repeat; the direction does not matter. Since you will feel all of these emotions at some point in your life, it is a fine practice to move through every one of them. Just keep moving quickly, *and don't let your thoughts (connected to the feeling) get stuck* in a thought loop, keeping you lodged in any one emotion for too long. When you decide to end the exercise, do so on an emotion you want to choose to stay with, then move to the centre of the wheel to see the symbol of Impermanence. This exercise helps you become master of the inevitable change of emotions due to Impermanence. Impermanence, like this exercise, is a gift. Savour these facts as a Reward.

And now, of course, do the Butterfly Hug! And give yourself a good, happy Reward for successfully choosing to do this exercise and investing the time in your well-being!

The Exercise: The Emotions Wheel

> When working with the Emotions Wheel, the goal is to become the Master of Changing Your Emotions.

First, be clear about your Intention in doing this exercise:

1. Set your Intentional goal. (Hint: It appears right before this sentence!)

2. Glance over the wheel and notice what event or thought comes to mind and the emotion on the wheel to which the Attending Thought leads you.

For example: *As I run through the wheel, the feeling* <u>*Optimistic*</u> *catches my eye. It does so because it is attached to my thoughts in this moment of how hopeful I am this book will change thousands of lives.*

I call this the *Attending Thought.* The Attending Thought does not have to occur to you before the emotion. For example, I may have first noticed the emotion *Worry* resonated with me ahead of this Attending Thought: *I am worried about my client getting here safely this afternoon, as it is a particularly nasty, cold, icy day here in Toronto.*

Alternatively, you may find the thought comes to mind first, and *then* the emotion on the wheel catches your eye. For example: *I just emptied my full garbage can again because the cleaners did not do their job, and I'm Angry with them!*

The protocol works either way: The emotion can trigger the thought, or the thought might make your eye notice the emotion on the wheel. Either way, you now have a thought and emotion to get you started.

3. Now that you have your starting point, pay close attention to the emotion. What does it feel like? Try to notice where you feel it in your body. You might even try to imagine where it resides in your brain. Spend a moment noticing how you experience the emotion or feeling.

Do your best not to judge it; just notice how it feels, and perhaps where you experience it. For example: *Worried; it's making me feel pretty crappy, and when I worry, if I check into my body, I seem to notice it in my throat. Yup, that's what Worried feels like!*

4. Select the next emotion on either side of the emotion you just spent a moment with in *Step 3*.

Ask yourself a question and construct a new thought that can move you to that next emotion. You may create a thought relative to the initial thought, or an entirely different thought. Either option is fine as the goal is in the *change*, not the thought. The goal in this step is to repeat the process of experiencing a new emotion, just like you did in *Step 3. The Thought is not the goal; the learning experiencing of changing to the new emotion is the goal.* Please reread that last sentence carefully. It is very important.

Here's a detailed example:

"I could go either way around the wheel—random choice, although one way may seem more rewarding than the other. But wait; I notice that I have slipped into judging these emotions, which is not a part of this exercise.

Here is what it looks like for me to go in either direction:

If I were to go up the list, the next emotion is Sad. For me to feel Sad, I can easily create the Attending Thought: I'm sad my 94-year-old client has physical challenges that make her a bit unstable on her feet, making it likely that she will bail on our appointment the moment she looks out the door, afraid she isn't up to the travel! *Yup, I can cause myself to feel Sad about her being homebound."*

Now I'll check in with myself: "Sad I seem to feel in my eyes, like I am about to cry. I can feel it sitting somewhere in the base of my brain messing with me! It still feels pretty crappy. Yes, I know what Sad feels like."

*Or, I could go the other way to Frustrated, and I might use a connected Attending Thought, or not. For example: "*This is my fault; I really should go to my geriatric clients, not have them come to me. Seriously, Todd, why have you not set up a program yet to travel to meet these clients! It's been on your to-do list for months and it's so frustrating that you have yet to make it happen. *I think I feel Frustration in my jaws; it feels like I'm clenching my teeth. Yes, I know what Frustration feels like." An unrelated Attending Thought might also move me to Frustration. For example: "*I am frustrated I have not fired my cleaning company and hired another!"

5. Continue to repeat this process, moving around the wheel. Pick a direction and move around the wheel *one* emotion/feeling at a time. Don't skip one even if it seems easier if you do. The goal is to become the *Master of Changing Your Emotions*, and if you jump an emotion or feeling on the list you get less Repetition of the desired change, which, of course, reduces one of the key components to creating neuroplastic change.

Feel the sensation of each emotion, and then move on to the next. Travel around the wheel as quickly as you want, moving along even the very second you feel the sensation of each emotion. It really is an awesome and very rewarding discovery when you notice that it is *you* who can change your emotions and feelings!

6. If you don't have time to go all the way around, or you're just too overwhelmed by the experience, stop the exercise on an emotion you would like to stay with, then move finally to the symbol for Impermanence in the centre of the wheel.

Be grateful for Impermanence; it is a gift that helps you savour the good feelings and emotions, and reminds you that the tougher ones won't last forever. Be grateful as you go to the stage of Reward. Notice how many steps you have moved in the list. Give you brain that Rewarding feeling of success. A good long Butterfly Hug is in order!

This exercise can be so powerful that I had the wheel printed on the back of my business cards so my clients could easily carry it with them and refer to it multiple times a day. Make your own cards and get all over this exercise! Carry them in your pockets and purse, and post the wheel on your computer screen and bathroom mirror. Have it readily available to remind you on a regular basis to practice becoming a Master of Changing Your Emotions—lots of Repetition!

The more you practice intentionally changing your emotions and feelings, the better practiced your brain becomes. When you find yourself in a tough situation or an emotion hits you hard, you will have built up the necessary brain muscles to make an emotional shift. Practice on this wheel often.

Becoming the Master of Changing Your Emotions is a learned skilled, and the Emotions Wheel exercise can be a very powerful tool in mastering this life-saving skill.

A Second Application for the Emotions Wheel

Now that you have learned how to use the Emotions Wheel to master your emotions, I want to introduce you to a second application. This strategy will help you at times when you are stuck in an emotion you would rather not feel, and would like to change that feeling to something better (notice the value judgement—I'll come back to this shortly).

Hop on the wheel at the emotion that corresponds to how you feel right now. Since the emotions on the wheel are very close, start moving around the wheel, shifting emotions—as in the first protocol—in a direction that will move you towards more positive ones. Shift through to an emotion you are prepared to stay with. It's a bit like riding a bike, once you get up a little momentum, you start to feel more stable. Once you settle on an acceptable emotion for this moment, move to the centre of the wheel and reflect on the gift of Impermanence. Move to the stage of Reward, then list your Gratitudes in the moment and give yourself a Butterfly Hug.

Now remember, this second application does require you to make a value judgment about the emotions, something I asked you *not* to do in the primary exercise. But of course if you weren't already aware that you didn't like this emotional state, you wouldn't engage the second application. Just be aware of your Intention to place value on the emotion this time around, so you don't unintentionally start judging emotions when you are working to become a Master of Changing Your Emotions. Because if you can accomplish that goal, with the second protocol available in more urgent situations, then maybe you'll be saying goodbye to panic attacks and unmanageable anxiety.

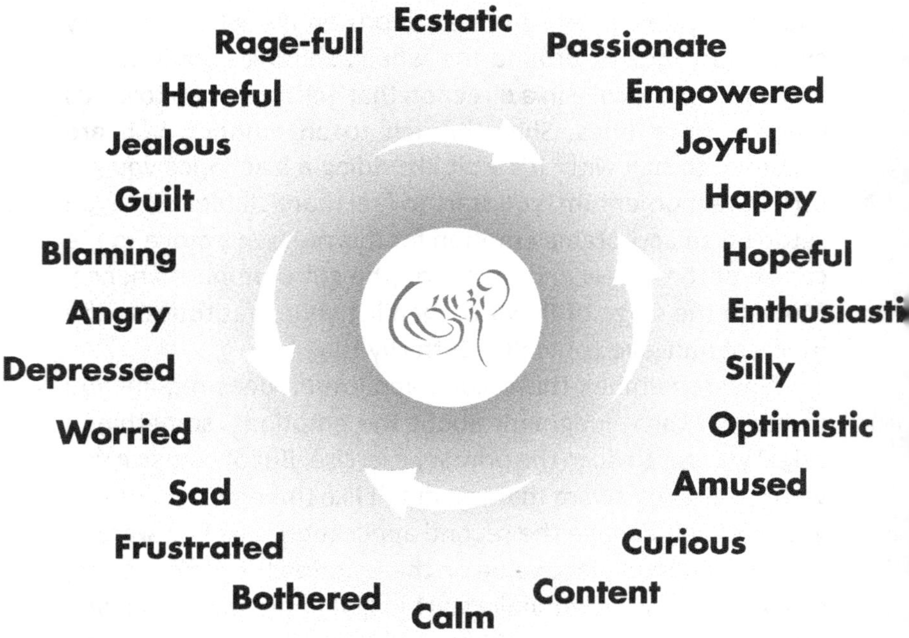

Ecstatic

Passionate

Empowered

Joyful

Happy

Hopeful

Enthusiasti

Silly

Optimistic

Amused

Curious

Content

Calm

Bothered

Frustrated

Sad

Worried

Depressed

Angry

Blaming

Guilt

Jealous

Hateful

Rage-full

Athletes are mentored by

GREAT COACHES

Who is your

THINKING COACH?

Chapter Twelve

NEUROPLASTIC MANTRAS

Reputations. They can often make or break someone, or something. And far too often reputations are built by distractors, and not based on direct experience.

I've had dogs since I was a child. Dogs offer unconditional love, and love is one of the best cures for stress and anxiety.

Many years ago I had a dog named Maggie. Maggie finally had to be put to sleep when the challenges of old age exceeded her capacity to enjoy her pampered life. She lived a glorious life of chasing balls, endless begging for bacon, and had this adorable but relentless habit of sticking her nose under your hand – regardless of what you were doing – to demand a pat, or ideally a cuddle.

At 50 pounds Maggie was no lap dog, but she couldn't fathom this. Maggie had no idea. After all, a lap was a warm comfy place where belly rubs were pretty much assured. Maggie slept every night with me, carefully positioned to keep my toes warms. She wasn't a morning type of girl, either. Even a morning pee could wait if Dad was willing to stay in bed and snuggle.

Maggie had a bright orange rubber ball she cherished. A

startling exception to sleep-ins would be made if anyone in our household was inclined to start my morning early and shout, "Ready, set, BALL!!" Then it was game on, and Dad had to immediately hop out of bed, pull on sweats, and head to the park. "Ball" became a verboten word in my household prior to coffee. It seemed Maggie knew about the three keys to neuroplastic change: Intention, Repetition and Reward. She would intentionally drop that orange ball on my feet, on my face, or anywhere she could to get my attention, relentlessly repeating her efforts until she got her reward. Darn smart dog she was!

And Maggie had a huge fat tail. She used it to tell us about her excitement or contentment. With seeming little effort, Maggie would lift her monster tail and let it fall on my beaten up old, pine wood floors. That warm "thump" could be heard through out the house. Often ensconced in the den next to the fireplace, Maggie would see dogs or monkeys on TV (she LOVED monkeys) and that monster tail would thump so fast and furious, it sounded like we had the drummer from Styx practicing on the second floor. Maggie's buddy Larry nicknamed her Thumper and the moniker stuck. Thumper was used most often when she was in uber love mode and that tail was playing a tune of joy!

When Maggie became a grand old lady, and her tail thumping had slowed to match her age, our city passed a law that Maggie had to move from her lifelong home or be put down. The nasty reputation of a few of other dogs of Maggie's breed had unjustly tainted *all* dogs of her breed, and the reputation was flat out wrong, and not good.

Maggie was a pitbull. The kindest, cutest, cuddliest, tail thumping puppy you would ever want to meet. A horrible a reputation had befallen her through no fault of her own.

We ignored the city and let Maggie live out her few last months in her lifelong home, feeding her tons of bacon, and succumbing to more cuddles then anyone can imagine, until the day came that Maggie's tail thumped no more.

Screw reputations. They can be so unfair.

In this chapter, I am going to offer you up a technique to build a personal, therapeutic mantra that can supercharge ARP Mantras.

Mantras are like Affirmations, but they are more carefully constructed. For some, mantras hold a reputation of being that new agey stuff that is all hocus pocus, yet experience has proven that reputation to be unjust. Hundreds of people worldwide have used this technique over the ages to transform their lives.

The concept of mantras comes from many ancient traditions, including the Vedic tradition. The Vedic tradition preceded Hinduism, and it's founders saw sound as a vibration. Believing that all things had vibrational energy, they learned that one could impact vibrations with vibrations. We now know that this belief is good science. All things at their most basic levels are composed of particles of energy with unique vibrations and frequencies. Unfortunately, this science is now used to develop weaponry, and various forms of energy (vibrations) can be modulated and directed at machinery or humans to disable or destroy them. We are going to use this power for good!

We also understand a bit more about the brain, and neuroplasticity. We are beginning to learn how to make change and rewire our neuro circuity. And now, so do you. By now you should understand how intentionally repeating a well crafted statement that makes you feel good will change your thoughts, and in turn, create a new experience of life for you when used with Intention, Repetition and Reward (IRR).

Too often we don't chose what we think, and when we let thoughts run unmonitored and unchecked, they embed physically into your neuro wiring. These thoughts then become the biology of our beliefs, and often they do not serve us well.

Thoughts held long enough and repeated often enough become beliefs. Beliefs become a solid set of neuro wiring in your brain.

Throughout this book, you have been asked to shift your beliefs and intentionally change and reshape your neurobiology. We have invited you to do this in multiple ways, though logical examination, re-framing, anthropomorphizing, Focal Point Meditations, Tapping and even diet and sleep.

A personal mantra is an intentional phrase or word crafted to embed a new positive belief. For all my techy friends, crafting a personal mantra that get results is just like writing and inserting a new line of code into a program. Written skillfully, it is often beautiful in its simplicity, and when inserted correctly, it dramatically impacts the outcome. Mantras are like inserting a line of code into your brain.

A mantra is not difficult to craft, but to create a mantra that is powerful and effective, is a science and an art.

I am going to walk you through the creation of your own mantra to help you manage anxiety and end panic attacks. This process can also be used to help you craft a new you, so you can become almost anything you really want to be. Adopting this skill can be a life changer on so many fronts!

Once we have crafted your mantra, I will walk you through the best practices to enable it to be part of how you create change in your life. Neither creating the personal mantra or implementing it is difficult.

Make a list of the top 5 to 10 times you felt calm, in control and or stress-free:

LIST A

	Event	Where were you?	Positive Feeling/ Sensation
i.e	a)Playing with my puppy	My favorite park	Silly and proud
	b)Cuddling with my partner	Home in bed	Love
	c) Working on my computer	Office	Confident
1.			
2.			
3.			
4.			
5.			
6.			
7.			
8.			
9.			
10.			

A. What Feeling/Sensation was strongest:

B. What Feeling/Sensation was repeated the most:

C. What one Feeling/Sensation would you like more of:

Now let's make a quick and short list of times your anxiety was at its most challenging:

LIST B

D. Which Feeling/Sensation would you most like to rid yourself of?

E. What is the OPPOSITE* feeling of what you answered in "D"?

C. What one Feeling/Sensation would you like more of:

- N.B. In earlier chapters, we learned that the opposite of love is not hate. The opposite of love is fear. That learning comes in very handy right about now!

Given this information, let's craft your personal mantra.

Use this simple formula:

"I AM ____'A____ (and) ____B'____ and ____'C'____.

So using my that formula my mantra might be:

"I AM love and worthy."

"I AM proud, confident and secure."

In your best handwriting, and in big letters, write out your personal mantra here:

____

____

____

Your personal mantra is your quick and easy go-to, and something you should memorize and make a habit. Say it often, say it loud, say it in your head, write it down, and chant it in the shower every morning. Say it in front of the mirror and share it with your pet. Notice how it makes you feel and relish in the positive sensations. Make this mantra a habit and your automatic go-to expletive!

It is really important that your mantra contains truth. "I am totally chill at all times," is not true for any of us. Yet for almost everyone "I am chill" is true at times in our lives, no matter how fleeting they may be. The game plan here is to magnify this truth by paying attention to it (IRR), and doing so in a way that it begins to engrain itself into your brain, becoming your new biology.

Now you have your basic personal mantra. Let's expand that mantra to be more directive and encompassing.

Here are some basic guidelines we need to maintain:

Your personal mantra MUST be:

- Present tense
- Affirming
- True (even if only a little bit)
- Easy to memorize
- Declarative, i.e. include, "I AM…"

Your personal mantra MAY be:

- Connected with positive spiritual beliefs
- Labelled in your current framework, i.e. as a "prayer"
- Incorporating your slang i.e., "I am a chill dude"
- A reminder of being love or receiving love*

* this element is so powerful it should be a MUST be!

Your personal mantra MUST NOT be:

- About "wanting" or any otherwise unfilled need or belief
- Negative/judgemental
- Past tense
- Phrased as a hope or expectation

Here are a few examples of mantras that I or clients have used that are powerful, well-crafted and have created change in my life or theirs.

A friend of mine who is a medical doctor uses this mantra:

> I am the gift of healing.
> I am a healer.
> I am healed.

A CEO of a multi-national tech firm uses this mantra:

> I am a leader.
> I am wise.
> I am kind.
> I am success.

A trauma survivor uses this mantra:

> I am loved.
> I have always survived.
> I am a survivor.
> I am strong.

A new mother who was on leave from her job as a CEO to care for her triplets uses this mantra:

> I am a CEO.
> I am a mom.
> I am love.
> I've got this!

(If you are like me, you are now imagining a bassinet of three screaming infants, piles of dirty diapers you have yet to have a chance to wash, blood shot eyes and three-day old shirt covered in baby puke. And yes, she's "got that!")

Here are a number of generic, but powerful mantras:

> I am resilient.
> I am positive.
> I embrace challenges.
> I honour outcomes.

I am love.
I am compassion.
I notice my intentions.
I am so grateful.

I know peace.
I am peace.
I create peace.

I am persistent.
I am resilient.
I am love.
I am loved.

Here is a mantra adapted from the "Prayer for Protection," by James Dillet Freeman:

The Light surrounds me;
The Light enfolds me;
The power of The Light protects me;
The presence of The Light watches over me
Wherever I am, The Light is!

An Olympic athlete who is a client uses this mantra:

I am an Olympian.
My body performs with precision.
My success is unstoppable.
I am THE winner.

Here is my personal mantra. It became a huge part of my life, as I battled cancer and underwent chemo and radiation. I used this mantra relentlessly over my year of battle, and I chanted it out loud during every radiation treatment. Today I am cured.

I am a child of God.
I am the love of Christ.
The love of Christ surrounds me.
The love of Christ heals me.
The love of Christ protects me.

Rewrite your personal mantra here:

____

____

____

Now go back and reflect on your lists A and B. In what areas would you like to expand your change? Write those out here:

____

List the top 3 areas in your life that, if changed, would lessen or alleviate your anxiety, and improve your quality of life:

1. ______________________________________

2. ______________________________________

3. ______________________________________

Beginning with your personal mantra as line one. Add two or three more lines to address one or two of the areas you listed in your top 3. Don't worry about not including all three. There is an interconnection in all of this, and addressing any one issue has a domino effect on the others.

Remember your guidelines list earlier. For example, if money (or lack of) is an element on your top 3, you can not say: "I am (or want to be) a millionaire." Instead you might say, "I AM financially successful."

Build your extended personal mantra here:

(insert your personal mantra)

____

____

____

How To Implement Your Mantra

Schedule your mantra's use, and make it a habit and part of your morning and evening rituals.

Create a physical trigger to remind you to use your mantra. Use simple reminders like sticky notes everywhere, wear your ring on a different finger, your watch on the other arm or disable your bio-metric password for your smartphone and set an alpha password with a short form of your mantra. Each time you notice these reminders, run your mantra a dozen times out loud or in your head. Begin and end your day by investing a short period (3-5 minutes) of repeating your mantra, ideally out loud and in front of a mirror.

List 3 additional physical triggers you can use to remind you to repeat your mantra:

1. ____

2. ____

3. ____

If you are a writer or enjoy journaling, write your mantra on paper. If you are an artist or love crafts, create plaques, images, or paintings of your mantra. Hang your mantra around your home or at work, and make it your screen saver.

List with detail, 1 or 2 creative things you can do create a physical reminder of your mantra:

1.

2.

Your mantra is your go-to thought replacement. Earlier chapters in the main book taught you about metacognition: the art of witnessing your thoughts. Metacognition is a critical skill in managing anxiety, as anxiety-based thoughts are always out of the future (fictional) that show up spontaneously, and we let them stick around to become ruminations, thought loops and worry. Remember, FEAR is an acronym for Fictional Events Appearing Real.

As you become Master of Choosing Your Thoughts by practising the earlier exercises in the main book, you can soon begin to automatically replace those FEAR-based thoughts at their initiation point with your mantra.

Be no less tenacious then my good old puppy Maggie with her orange rubber ball!

Okay, grab your sweat pants my friends because it is: Ready, Set, BALL!!

Life is not about "becoming";
it is about

UN-BECOMING

So you can be what you were
created for in the first place:
Love.

Chapter Thirteen

HAPPINESS FOR THE LONG TERM

Let's Make This Stick!

Perhaps by now you really understand why some or all of these wonderful therapeutic modalities such as CBT, meditation and psychotherapy have worked for you, and how much of a difference each has made. Many, if not all of these approaches can help different people to varying degrees. After all, none of us are wired the same. And because we are all different, some approaches make more sense to us than others, and have more or less impact on our well-being, and in particular, on ending our panic attacks and helping us manage our anxiety.

A wise approach to solving any challenge is to consider the common denominator between different occurrences of the problem. What things happen every time the challenge arises? This is a helpful approach whether we are perfecting a sporting activity or trying to bring about world peace! Most often, there is something (or things) in every instance that seems to tip the apple cart.

In the challenge of ending panic attacks and managing anxiety, I explained in Chapter Five, "The Path of Least Resistance," the common denominator that I have repeatedly found holding people back: They try to fight their anxiety and panic attacks. It is so critical that you remove this common denominator, I will end this practical manual by asking you to go back and reread Chapter Five.

Please.

As a therapist and an anxiety specialist, I see people struggling to let go of a core belief (even when it no longer serves them) that leads them to fight their anxiety. Most of us, and even many mental health professionals, believe that anxiety is painful and bad, and that consequently it needs to be fought to the death! After all, it has brought us, and those who know and love us, so much harm. Our intuitive response is understandable, and hardwired: Fight this thing off! We have a very hard time letting go of the desire to fight our anxiety, even when painful experience ought to teach us that it doesn't work.

In treatment sessions, I listen carefully to a client's language. I often hear phrases such as, "I think I may have licked this thing—I had an awesome week!" Specifically, I notice language like "licked it," or "beat it." Here, the ever-important Reward is present (following Intention and Repetition), yet it implies having won what is still framed in the client's mind as a *fight*.

Our language, when we are not paying attention, can be a key indicator of our core beliefs. It is very difficult to monitor your own spontaneous language objectively. This is why it can be so helpful to engage a therapist or anxiety specialist to coach you though your anxiety management. They are trained to carefully guide you through the process of changing the core beliefs that keep you bracing yourself for a fight when stress hormones start flooding your body.

Hundreds of folks have successfully applied the Anxiety Release Protocol on their own. Most often, it is people who are so sick and tired of being sick and tired from their anxiety that they read this manual with strong Intention, and they carefully Repeat the techniques of ARP, each and every step, with great care, reveling in every milestone, big and small.

Even if you are only a little bit committed, I have seen many like you profoundly change their anxiety levels once they really "get it," and "it" is Chapter Five. So one more time: Before you dig deeper into changing your life for the better, go back and reread Chapter Five and stop fighting your anxiety!

The Disconnect: A Second Common Denominator

I have worked with hundreds, if not thousands, of people and helped them end panic attacks and manage anxiety. As you can imagine, we get to know each other pretty well in doing so. Along the way, I have discovered a question that is important to answer in order to effect long-term relief and prevent you from reverting back to old behaviours: *Why did your brain (Homer, in particular) wind up wired in such a way that your fight or flight response overworks?*

The answer to that is different for everyone, and a gifted therapist can help you answer it for yourself. But in that process of discovery, my clients and I have consistently come across another key piece of the puzzle: When they stop and really look at their lives, they recognize that they are not living according to their *deepest values*. This is not usually by choice; life and circumstances landed them in a place where what they do and how they act are out of sync with the person they know themselves to be.

You might call "deep values" the "truth" of who you are, your "soul purpose" or your "*raison d'etre*." There may very well be a disconnect between your deepest values and the reality of how you are living your life and relationships. It seems that a frequent response to this kind of disconnect is high levels of anxiety and even panic. On a more existential level, your brain may seem to know it needs to be in flight mode, fleeing an existence that is out of alignment with your best self.

So how do you recognize this disconnect, and what can you do about it?

Over the Long Term

There has never been, nor will there ever be, someone just like you. Even identical twins do not grow up to be the same person; they have differences. You are unique.

How you became who you are is a deep, complex and long story. Part of what makes you unique is that your story is not identical to anyone else's.

As you've learned in this book, we have the ability to stimulate our brains in ways that lay down new neuronal connections that give us desired responses in any given situation. By now, you should understand both how and why you can choose and change your responses by changing this wiring.

It is by recalling and understanding the complexity of our stories that we can use various techniques to ultimately rewrite our stories in our brains, and to ensure that if we regress in a moment when we have failed to be present—a clear awareness of being in our surroundings, that is—then we still find ourselves moving towards our better, desired outcome.

Wait, what?! Did you just say rewrite our stories? Is this some kind of brainwashing you are suggesting?!

In a word, no.

Remember: You are not your brain; you are a combination of your brain and some sort of energy (call it your soul, spirit or universal energy), and when these two are integrated you call it your *mind*. Your brain is just another organ in your body (a *really* important one, but nonetheless, an organ).

Remember, too, that your brain processes events in your sleep, in particular during REM sleep. That process is not always perfect, but when it is, you gather up all the bits and pieces of your day in your brain and store them like a book, with a beginning, middle and an end, in your hippocampus. Then, if you reflect on a memory, even the horrible ones, your mind knows there is an "end" to that part of the story, enabling you to relax. If this process is not done well, or completely—as is often the case if you're suffering sleepless nights due to elevated anxiety—you can trip over components of these stories that have been left unfiled in your brain. This can trigger panic. Your amygdala kicks into overdrive to help protect you from a piece of a story that it recognizes as unresolved and therefore still potentially a threat to your well-being.

Working with a good therapist, you can unpack your most informative stories, collect up all those bits and pieces and file them neatly away. In doing so, you rewrite the stories in your brain's filing system, removing the trigger for your brain's default response of panic. So your stories remain, and your memories remain; they are just sorted and filed in a way that they can inform you, not harm you. (And if this still sounds to you like brainwashing, consider that what you're really doing here is finishing a process that would have been completed had you just gotten a decent night's sleep. You are just empowering your brain to do what it should have done in the first place!)

Go for Gold

Old habits and beliefs die hard. Even after mastering a new skill or a new way of doing or being something, there is always some residual wiring that, if not addressed, you could inadvertently revert to using.

The clients I know who mastered the ARP technique but didn't put in place an ongoing way to monitor what their brain is up to are the ones who wind up back in my office months or years later puzzled as to why, once again, they are experiencing panic attacks or a crazy level of anxiety. ARP is a protocol that relieves symptoms and helps to rewire your brain. ARP is not designed to uncover and shift core beliefs.

This is where a regular visit with a therapist might be in order. ARP is a powerful tool used by therapists globally. You might have mastered it on your own with this book, but the deeper work around values and sometimes the causes of anxiety is the skilled work a therapist can help you accomplish. If your anxiety is a result of PTSD, this is a good example of where the causes need to be worked on with modalities beyond ARP.

I really like to think of a therapist as a brain coach.

If you loved playing golf, and your game was good but not good enough to beat your boss, who crushed you every time you played, or if you were a world-class athlete and you really wanted to win gold at the next Olympics, what would you do?

Most of us would hire the best golf pro or Olympic coach we could find and afford.

A therapist or "brain coach" can teach you how to think in ways that get you to nail that hole-in-one or win the gold, so to speak. They have spent years training to be a good therapist, and most have played the anxiety game themselves and mastered a good many parts of it (most therapists, to complete training and become licensed, have had to do hundreds of hours of personal therapy).

On top of all this training, the experienced ones have spent hundreds of hours working with people, many of whom might have faced the same types of challenges or problems as you. They bring to your sessions the stories of how these hundreds of people have tried and both failed at and mastered their challenges. Good therapists are not just well-trained in a broad array of therapies, they are a repository of stories, coaching experiences and life experiences. They bring all of that to *your* game. The good ones know how to help you achieve your goals, and are committed to being as effective for you as any golf pro or Olympic coach.

Pick your therapist as carefully as you would pick a coach to help you win an Olympic gold. Above all, find someone you can connect with, someone you trust and admire, and ideally, someone who has "been there, done that."

I have clients I have been seeing for years. They came to me to end their panic attacks and ease their anxiety, and they succeeded. And they come back to check in as often as we feel is necessary to ensure their bad habits don't return.

Once the techniques of the ARP are mastered, we can usually taper off the frequency of our sessions. I meet these clients—whom I call my Anxiety Masters—about four times a year and whenever they are facing big challenges or changes in their life. This long-term plan ensures that the work we did, the skills they mastered, isn't forgotten or allowed to slide enough to cause fresh problems.

Most importantly, therapy provides a safe place for you to objectively review *you*, and take note of whether *you* are doing *life*, or *life* is doing *you!* Therapy is a place you can make certain you are connecting with your best self rather than letting life push you away from the deep values that make you the person you want to be.

Are you doing life, or is it doing you?

I honestly love my clients. Together we have retold countless stories, healed old wounds, forged new trails, cried, and laughed. They *and* I learn to be better and happier people because of our time together.

So embrace Intention and go find your Olympic brain coach! Trust me: Over time you will create a unique and powerful alliance that will change your world for the better, help you keep that change you worked so hard to create, and maintain your happiness for the long term.

When you cross the

DARKEST VALLEYS

you will find the

BRIGHTEST MEADOWS

There are short cuts.
Use a guide.

Appendix

ANXIETY RELEASE PROTOCOL OVERVIEW

Depathologize

You are not broken or damaged. A part of your brain, your amygdala (your fight/flight centre), is simply overworking.

The symptoms you feel are a direct result of elevated cortisol and adrenaline.

Fundamentals and Reframing

We began this manual with the story of two cavemen, Brad and Larry, Larry being the guy who was always prepared for the worst. Larry survived to pass on his DNA and ultimately we, his descendants, became an apex (top of the heap) species because of our ability to worry and plan.

FEAR-based (Fictional Events Appearing Real) thinking is a blessing, as it keeps you safe, and a curse because it can cause you undue anxiety. When you learn to accept your evolutionary inheritance for the blessing it is, you empower yourself to work with and manage your anxiety.

Thought loops (ruminations) happen when you get stuck in these FEAR-based thoughts. Remember: *Just because you have a thought, that doesn't mean you have to keep it!* Choosing your thoughts is a learned skill.

You can change your brain and its wiring. This is thanks to something called neuroplasticity. It allows anything you do with Intention, Repetition and Reward to create change.

Reframe your understanding of the physical expressions of panic and anxiety, such as recognizing that an elevated heartbeat and sweating is nothing more than the direct result of the elevation of two hormones, adrenaline and cortisol. These feelings would result whether it was your amygdala that triggered their release or if they were injected into your bloodstream.

Anthropomorphization

In order to work with your anxiety instead of fight it, characterize it: Visualize a well-intentioned character that sits in your amygdala with his or her hands on the controls that release adrenaline and cortisol. Choosing the name of a character you can embrace is important. Often, cartoon characters such as Homer or Bugs work well.

Understand that Homer's job is to protect you and that he wants two things: to get your attention and to create an environment that keeps you safe. Using the techniques in Chapter Five, give Homer precisely what he wants, thus shutting off his need to release the hormones that give you unpleasant physical symptoms.

Skills Acquisition

Preparing Your Brain for Change

You would not expect a gasoline-powered car to run well if you filled its tank with diesel. Similarly, your brain is a complex piece of machinery and it needs not only the right fuel to function, but optimum fuel if you expect it to change.

Using the diet guidelines in Chapter Four, easily fuel your brain in ways that help you create permanent change in your ways of thinking.

Focal Point Meditation

You need to learn how to become a Master of Choosing Your Thoughts in order to avoid getting stuck in thought loops, and in order to choose thoughts that bring you a feeling of calm and peace rather than anxiety. Choosing your thoughts is a learned skill.

Cardiac Coherence and Pranayama

Cardiac Coherence is a form of deep breathing that helps your heart and lungs work together to create a relaxed state of balance in your body. Integrate Pranayama, a form of yogic breathing, for greater beneficial outcomes, including a lowering of hormones, like cortisol and adrenaline, that effect your stress and relaxation levels.

Gratitude Therapy

Rewiring your brain to intuitively see the cup as half full, or even more than half full, is a key to managing anxiety and living a happy life.

Using the basic tools of Gratitude Therapy, you can develop

neuronal networks that make your brain generate thoughts that notice Gratitude. Thoughts of Gratitude and being in a place of Gratitude is almost the opposite of anxiety!

Cognitive Behavioural Therapy for ARP

CBT is a proven way to help change your thinking process and in turn change your thoughts so you have a more positive and happier response to people and situations.

Tapping, or Emotional Freedom Technique (EFT)

Tapping integrates Western medicine's Exposure Therapy with Eastern medicine's understanding of hormone management through acupuncture/acupressure. Use EFT to rewire your brain and desensitize your response to experiences that precipitate your anxiety.

Emotions Wheel

We use meditation techniques to become Master of Choosing our Thoughts. The Emotions Wheel helps us to become Master of Changing Our Emotions.

A second application of the Emotions Wheel is to help you shift out of an unpleasant emotion or feeling when you catch yourself ruminating or stuck in a thought loop.

Neuroplastic Mantras

This powerful technique can supercharge the ARP by creating a regular repetitive neuronal trigger that improves metacognition and favourable neuronal wiring.

Psychotherapy and Treatment

Commit to working with a skilled therapist. This will enable you to do the longer-term, necessary work to discover why your brain is so heavily defaulted to the evolutionary response. By participating in practical therapies such as Eye Movement Desensitization and Reprocessing (EMDR), hypnosis, CBT and others, you can undo this default programing to ensure that you do not regress to your old ways of thinking and habits.

Psychotherapy and Treatment

[illegible]

THOUGHTS

held long and repeated
become beliefs.

BELIEFS

become neuronal wiring
in your brain.

Thoughts are your

BIOLOGY

being made.

Epilogue

The very thought of being trapped in a highly pressurized aluminum tube hurtling through space at hundreds of miles per hour almost a mile above the planet's surface can trigger anxiety in many people!

Yet there I was, aboard a five-hour commercial flight heading home from a speaking engagement in Vancouver, Canada. The flight was about three-quarters of its way to my hometown of Toronto, and we were just past Winnipeg, a bitter cold city at that time of year, perched in the middle of Canada on the edge of its vast, frozen prairies.

I reflected on an earlier part of my day.

As part of my commitment to living as stress-free a life as I can, I always arrive at airports early. Really early.

Well before the crowds had arrived at the airport that evening, I breezed through check-in and security, found myself a comfy corner by the gate and cracked open a good book.

Through a combination of charm and good planning I can often score myself an upgrade, or at least a bulkhead seat that saves me spending the five hours closely examining my kneecaps. That evening, Dan was the name of the gentleman who checked me in. (*Always* look at name tags and use people's names, it makes them feel appreciated!). Dan was one of those guys who clearly lived in the gym when he was not at work, and it looked like his airline had issued him a suit that was a few sizes too small. I noticed his tattoos peeking out of his collar and shirtsleeve, and intentionally remarked on how cool they looked. Dan succumbed to my friendly chatter and I found myself in the aisle seat, just behind the first-class bulkhead, with lots of wiggle room and no neighbours. Score!

So there we were, a few hours into the flight. From my seat I could peek through the curtain that separated the cattle class from the well-travelled passengers who had likely redeemed a pile of hard-earned points to get there. I had a clear view of seat 5C and could tell the woman sitting in that seat was becoming agitated and uncomfortable.

Suddenly, Madeline (I would hear her name soon enough) in 5C decided that this pressurized tube was likely to explode, scattering us all into little bits over the prairies. No doubt, that visual was all she could imagine when her "Homer" started screaming in her head like a banshee from hell. She suddenly matched that scream with one of her own, startling everyone around her, and bolted towards the emergency exit. As a general rule, one should *not* go for the emergency exit when at an altitude of 36,000 feet and a speed of 512 mph. But as you now know, the executive functioning part of our brain is mostly offline when we think we are in extreme danger, and clearly Madeline had not thought her personal flight plan through.

Diminutive Madeline made it only to row two. Mark, the onboard purser, who looked as if he might have been Dan's inspiration at the gym, intercepted her. He wrapped his massive arms around a totally freaked out, four-foot-eight, 98-pound Madeline, and carried her squirming and squealing like a feral kitten back to her seat.

The rest of the cabin crew converged on poor Madeline, and the show of force (which was surprisingly as compassionate as it was forceful) calmed her enough to get her sobbing frame belted back into her seat, no doubt only moments before Mark or the crew decided that more serious restraints were required.

A small chime rang through the cabin and a very calm voice said, "Ladies and gentlemen, if there is a doctor on board, would you please present yourself to the cabin crew by ringing your call attendant button." A few buttons behind me chimed. The aircraft banked hard. The captain had quickly decided that Madeline might best be served by cooling off in lovely, frozen Winnipeg. (Don't get me wrong; I love my country, and even Winnipeg. In fact, it has a stunning Human Rights Museum I would love to visit, just not in that moment, and certainly not in February!)

From the very best of the cheap seats, I was watching all of this unfold, and I knew exactly what was happening (just as you do now). Madeline was having a massive panic attack.

I am not a doctor. And although a doctor carrying a syringe full of horse tranquilizer would have solved the cabin crew's problem, I felt called to help Madeline before she got drugged or had to go one more round with Purser Mark. The flight attendant was walking past and I flagged her down. "Hi, my name's Todd. I'm a therapist and specialist in panic attacks. I saw this all unfold. I've got this, just give me a few minutes." I didn't wait for a response and headed up to first class.

Mark was still looming over Madeline. She was sobbing. Her seat companion was being of no help, and Purser Mark, likely an experienced parent of a difficult toddler (or at least a lover of feral cats), was doing his best to soothe Madeline while making it clear he was not going to tolerate another escape attempt. He was trying his best, but as you and I well know, no one in the history of calming down has ever calmed down by being told to calm down.

"Hey, Mark," I said, tapping his shoulder, "give me a moment here with Madeline. I can fix this." Mark eyed me up and down, then stepped aside, his gaze darting between his charge, Madeline, and me, the unknown interloper. The flight attendants behind me settled concerned folks back into their seats. The seatbelt sign turned on to encourage everyone to join Madeline in a safely strapped-in position. The plane stopped banking and settled into a slow descent.

"Hi, Madeline. I'm Todd. I used to get these panic attacks too and know how to end them. Is this your first? Have you ever woken up dead from one?" You and I know it was likely not her first, and that she had obviously not woken up dead from one, but I was going to slam dunk the Anxiety Release Protocol as quickly as I could!

I continued. "These feel pretty awful, but at least it's not dangerous and they always go away. Haven't they always gone away? Would you like me to take this one off your hands?" I smiled as warmly as I could, and reached out for her hand.

Madeline quickly accepted my hand and I squeezed it gently. Slam dunking the ARP meant using all its tools, including humour: "Madeline, I bet if you look inside your head there are some thoughts spinning around like crap in a toilet that won't flush down! Let's flush those thoughts; they are not really helpful right now! Here, let me show you how. Want to see some magic? Tap here." And I began to tap on Madeline's Karate Chop point.

"You know, this meltdown isn't *really* a panic attack; it's just a hormone called cortisol rushing through your body. Can you feel it in your hands and head? It's making your heart beat fast too, isn't it?"

Madeline nodded.

"Here, Madeline, you tap here on your hand. This makes that cortisol go away and you will feel better." I was straightforward, warm, kind and in control, and that felt safe to Madeline. She complied and I asked her to play a game, to repeat what I said and tap on her body where I tapped on mine.

And we were off. After a few false starts and a little encouragement, I tapped our Madeline back to a state of reasonable calm.

You know how this went down (oops—no pun intended there!): Madeline was guided through a crash course (ok, I'm getting too punny!) in ARP, her cortisol level dropped, and we engaged in a wonderful conversation about anything *but* flying.

"Excuse me, sir." It was Purser Mark. He motioned for me to stand and step forward. "The captain is preparing for an emergency landing in Winnipeg. If you tell me you can keep her calm for the next few hours to Toronto, he's willing to head us back home."

"Yes, Mark, I got this. But I want an upgrade to first class and a seat next to Madeline."

Mark chuckled and said, "Yeah, that was the plan."

Madeline's seat partner willingly moved and I slid in next to her as the plane banked again and turned back towards Toronto. "It looks like they might actually spoil us from here on in. Mind if I milk this for some extra goodies now that I'm out of the cheap seats?"

Madeline laughed, and I spent the next 90 minutes making a new friend and chatting about how cool it would be if she learned to shift all that energy of her meltdown into a superpower! Madeline loved Wonder Woman, so she was totally on-board. I continued to carefully support Madeline as our captain ever so gently took us home and settled the big bird onto the runway in Toronto.

The Anxiety Release Protocol works.

Time and time again, I and therapists trained in the ARP have coached people just like you, our passenger Madeline, ER patient Becky, football star Lars and bride Sarah back to a life where panic attacks are gone and anxiety levels are reasonable, and relative to the situation. (Notice there was not a fighting word in that statement!)

Even if your anxiety and stress have not reached the panic-attack level, ARP is a proven strategy to help you live a life free from extreme stress by teaching you how to manage your "Homer" (the fight/flight part of your brain), choose your thoughts, avoid ruminating, manage your emotions and do life, instead of letting life do *you!*

I encourage you to use this guide book as a regular resource, and if you still need support and coaching, because this stuff is more fun together and sometimes a bit challenging alone, reach out to a local ARP-trained therapist, or even give my office a call. You deserve a life free of panic attacks and full of joy and happiness. ARP has turned around the lives of so many.

Now it's your turn.

***

THANK YOU!
(It never hurts to end with Gratitude)

It was such a relief to turn my life around many years ago. I'm truly thankful for each and every experience and trial that ultimately prompted me to figure this all out.

And more importantly, I am thankful to my hundreds of clients over the years who travelled on this journey with me. We put this whole program together and very quickly we started to see profound changes. We have all learned so much through our time and conversations together. I count these relationships as some of the most valuable relationships I have ever had.

I became a therapist because I wanted to be able to help others in a bigger way than all of my other jobs had afforded me. I believe I am pretty lucky, if not blessed, to be wired for empathy and compassion. Creating the ARP, a program that has changed the lives of so many, has been incredibly rewarding. I hope you will become part of the ever-growing group of people who use this method to help end their panic attacks and manage their anxiety. And if you do, please let others know about your success and send them our way.

This book can be a solution or a great start to a stress-free, panic-free life. My wish for you is that the ARP can help you transform your anxiety into your superpower, like it has for so many. We hope to change as many lives as possible, and for that we need your help to spread the word. Above all, do not let this book become one of the many self-help books that quickly devolves into a "shelf-help" book that never helps anyone. The book you are holding has proven truly transformation for so many, so please, pass it along to a friend and spread the love!

www.ingramcontent.com/pod-product-compliance
Lightning Source LLC
Chambersburg PA
CBHW060323030426
42336CB00011B/1181

* 9 7 8 1 7 7 8 2 3 3 5 0 0 *